GOT TO BE
SOMETHING HERE

GOT TO BE SOMETHING HERE

•

THE RISE OF THE MINNEAPOLIS SOUND

ANDREA SWENSSON

Foreword by Jellybean Johnson

University of Minnesota Press
Minneapolis
London

Published by the University of Minnesota Press
111 Third Avenue South, Suite 290
Minneapolis, MN 55401-2520
http://www.upress.umn.edu

ISBN 978-1-5179-1199-7

A Cataloging-in-Publication record for this book is available from the Library of Congress.

Printed in the United States of America on acid-free paper

The University of Minnesota is an equal-opportunity educator and employer.

26   25   24   23   22   21   8   7   6   5   4   3   2   1

For North Minneapolis and Rondo

CONTENTS

·

FOREWORD

Jellybean Johnson

My mom moved me to Minneapolis in 1968. I was about to turn thirteen years old. The gangs in Chicago were really bad—they were starting to recruit me, and she wasn't happy, so she packed me and my little brothers up and moved us here.

It was culture shock because in Chicago, it was Black. Prime example: Black radio there was twenty-four hours a day. When my mom moved me here in '68, Black radio was only four hours a day. It was like one to five in the afternoon on KUXL. It forced me to listen to the white radio stations, and that's when I got into the white rock—Three Dog Night, Rare Earth, Black Sabbath, Cream, all those. I'm sure that developed my musical taste as I got older.

I met Morris Day because we had a mutual friend, a guitar player named Ronald Reinhardt. We were all about thirteen or fourteen years old, and Ronald was into Jimi Hendrix. He had the Jimi look. We were in a band with Ronald, and we decided we were gonna have two drummers, so we did that for a minute. I used to hike my drums over to Morris's house, which was like fourteen blocks away, and we would play in his mom's living room side by side damn near all day, learning David Garibaldi beats from Tower of Power.

When we started Flyte Tyme it was me, David "Batman" Eiland, Terry Lewis, Robert "Big Bob" Johnson, Robert "Bird" Martin, Jimmie "Chipmunk" Anderson, Joey Karriem, Gary McCray, and Cynthia

Johnson of "Funkytown" fame. David Eiland's dad was a vice president at Pillsbury, and he owned a big house on the corner of Plymouth and Upton, and that's where Flyte Tyme—all ten, eleven, twelve pieces of us—would rehearse every single day. And then we found out about Grand Central shortly after that. We found out because Prince moved in with André Cymone—they were right up on Russell.

When I got to be fourteen or fifteen, my mom would let me do certain things because she knew I was heavily into music. There would be movies at midnight at the Skyway Theater in downtown Minneapolis. Now, mind you, in the Black neighborhood we had a neighborhood theater—actually, where Prince played his first concert, the Capri Theater. That was our neighborhood theater. And all the Black people would go there to see all the Blaxploitation movies, you know, *Coffy* and *The Mack* and *Shaft*. But to see something like *Woodstock* you had to go somewhere where there was gonna be white people. That's the Skyway.

So I caught the bus one night, late, and I went down for the midnight show. And I get in there, and it's packed: it's jam-packed. I get like halfway down the rows, and I find a seat. And maybe a couple rows up from me, there's two big Afros. Now we were probably the only three Black people in this whole theater, and it turns out that those two Afros belonged to Prince and André Cymone. I remember sitting there watching at the end of *Woodstock* when Jimi was playing "The Star-Spangled Banner" and watching André's and Prince's reactions. I had never seen them like that. I had never heard sounds come out of a guitar like that. And it all just blew me away.

That was the first moment I realized that they were into rock and roll too. And what cemented it was I saw Grand Central maybe six, seven months later. We played a gig together, and Prince had a white guitar strap. So I said, "Yeah, he learned." I'm sure that affected Prince greatly. And it showed: like with his first records, you hear the rock songs like "Bambi" on the *Prince* album. All that comes from our upbringing.

I hung out at The Way a lot. Just like the late-night showing of *Woodstock* at the Skyway, they had late-night dances down there. The Way had a badass band, the Family. The original Family. Pierre

Lewis was like thirteen years old playing the organ, and they had Joe Lewis, Sonny Thompson, Randy Barber. They were amazing; they were really amazing. And then Spike Moss would throw those big festivals every year in North Commons. All the local bands would have our asses out there 'til late at night. There'd be thousands of people out there in the park. And the police didn't bother us. There's no way in hell you could do that now. There's no way.

The Minneapolis Sound was all about bringing the Black and white players together. Prince figured that out; he made sure he had white people in his band. With Flyte Tyme, because of the discrimination, we could play only Black sororities, the occasional party, or out at the Thunderbird Hotel in Bloomington.

But Flyte Tyme got lucky one time. We were like fifteen, sixteen years old, and the Flame Bar downtown on Nicollet hired us. We were playing down at the Flame Bar from Tuesday through Saturday. They had two sides: one side was funk, and the other side was country. One night we were just messing around because wasn't nobody there, and we got off stage and Robert Martin, who we call Bird, said, "Damn, we sound bad tonight. We sound like a bunch of jellybeans." He looked at me and said "Jellybean Johnson!" Everybody fell out laughing. The next day he comes, and he has this T-shirt with "Jellybean" on it. And I've been Jellybean Johnson ever since.

The last time I was with Prince, in January 2016, we were at Paisley until three or four in the morning, and he and Morris had this two-hour conversation. Morris was all a mess. They hadn't spoken in years like that. And Morris came on the bus and told us what Prince had said, and it was all Black Lives Matter, Black Lives Matter. The first thing out of Prince's mouth was, "Morris, they're killing us. Why are they killing us?" He wrote a song about that, about Freddie Gray: "Baltimore." Numerous incidents had already happened by then.

And now, since he's passed, even more. George Floyd, he was an older Black man. That could have been me. And the sad thing about it is that we're already in this pandemic, people have already lost their jobs, people are struggling—especially people of color—just to put food on the table. And so they call the police on him about a fake twenty-dollar bill?

So I will never forget this. I'm sixty-three years old, and I was around for the riots in '68, I seen all that as a little shorty. But to see this again in the fourth quarter of my life is just unbelievable. It really woke me up, especially to systemic racism. If 2020 did anything, it really woke me up to what's going on.

NOTE TO THE PAPERBACK EDITION

In the four years since this book was first published, the Twin Cities of Minneapolis and St. Paul have continued to reckon with racial inequities and social divides. When George Floyd, a forty-six-year-old Black man, was murdered by white police officer Derek Chauvin on the corner of Thirty-eighth Street and Chicago Avenue in South Minneapolis on May 25, 2020, it set off an awakening about police brutality that was felt around the globe and an uprising that echoed the unrest that forever altered North Minneapolis in the late-1960s.

The local history that I studied while researching this book has never felt so relevant to what is unfolding now before our eyes, and my hope is that more Minnesotans, especially white Minnesotans like myself, will take the time to learn more holistically about the Black musicians we love to celebrate. In order to truly understand the significance of their accomplishments and contributions, it's essential that we honor their full humanity by acknowledging the pain, hardship, and violence that white supremacy inflicts on all Black people, regardless of whether they're still grinding away at local clubs or have been inducted into the Rock and Roll Hall of Fame.

—Andrea Swensson, January 2021

.

PROLOGUE

"Prince is a human being. All these cats are."
—Sonny Knight

DOZENS OF BOOKS have already been written about Prince, his lasting imprint on American rock music, and his roots in Minneapolis. If there is one thing to take away from all of those unauthorized biographies—aside from the fact that they contain multitudes of conflicting details, mostly because Prince rarely allowed his interviews to be recorded—it is that so many of these narratives are delivered with a sense of surprise. How did this guy even exist? How did he manage to emerge on the national scene fully formed, like a Martian who was beamed down to teach us about the joys of lace and the virtues of squealing guitar solos, electronic drum samples, and the color purple? In the words of Dick Clark, who introduced a shy young Prince Rogers Nelson to the world on *American Bandstand* in 1979, "This isn't the kind of music that comes out of Minneapolis!"

If we choose to believe that, then we would also choose to believe that there weren't any artists playing funk, soul, R&B, and jazz music in Minnesota prior to Prince's reign. We would choose to believe that Prince couldn't possibly have been exposed to the deep grooves and electric sizzles of black music in a lily-white, Lutheran, Scandinavian metropolis like Minneapolis. And we would choose to believe that a boundary-smashing artist who channeled music from both white and black worlds is an inexplicable anomaly and not an observant and inquisitive human being who drew from his experiences growing up in both North and South Minneapolis to make simultaneously unifying and subversive art.

The truth is that the Twin Cities of Minneapolis and St. Paul were then and continue to be deeply segregated. And the more we treat Prince like a singular creature who must have been beamed down to Earth, because he couldn't have possibly emerged from an actual place, the more we help to erase the generations of influential jazz, gospel, soul, R&B, and funk musicians who first made it possible for African Americans to earn a living making music in Minnesota and contributed to the ongoing evolution of sound that eventually enraptured a young Mr. Nelson.

Prince and his teenage comrades Morris Day, André Cymone, Jimmy Jam, and Terry Lewis were the products of Minneapolis. They were raised by parents who were deeply rooted in the community, both musically and socially, and they were exposed to legions of talented predecessors in the R&B and soul community who inspired them and gave them the drive to get better and better. They were the products of a school integration program that bussed North Minneapolis kids to the south side, exposing them to mainstream classic rock, and white fashion and culture in the process, and they were the products of more than a decade of community building and social services that were developed to give young minority students a creative outlet on the north side. When we talk about Prince and his peers blazing a new trail in music that blurred genre and race lines, we can't fully appreciate that narrative without drawing lines across a map of Minneapolis and St. Paul and connecting them to the previous twenty years of African American struggles and triumphs in the Twin Cities.

To truly tell the story of the Minneapolis Sound, we must tell the story of Minneapolis.

As a music journalist working in the Twin Cities, I have become leery of the overwhelming whiteness of our historical narratives. We talk about Bob Dylan and the time he spent in Hibbing and Dinkytown; we talk about the Castaways and the Trashmen and their garage rock peers who were catapulted onto the national arena by Soma

Records. And then, like a rock skipping across Lake Minnetonka, we pick up the story in the early '80s with the rise of Prince, the Replacements, Hüsker Dü, the Suburbs, Soul Asylum, and so on. But what about those years in between? What was happening in the seventeen years between when Dylan left Minnesota in 1961 and Prince released his debut album, *For You*?

Unfortunately, I know firsthand just how easy it can be for the media to focus on the prominent white narratives and turn a blind eye to our communities of color. I have heard the frustrations from artists of color in the community, some of whom have been toiling away out of the limelight for twenty years or more. We like to pride ourselves on being a progressive place. The best biking city in the nation! And one of the most literate, too! But in recent years we've been forced to confront some ugly truths about our metropolis. We have some of the worst racial disparities in the nation when it comes to income, education, and housing. We knowingly bulldozed poor communities of color to build freeways and give suburbanites easy access to downtown jobs and nightlife. And our police force struggles with the same issues of unnecessary force and racial bias that have been plaguing the rest of the nation.

When I started to research this book, it quickly became apparent that this story is not limited to the albums that were recorded and the shows that were played by these fantastic bands. This story is so much bigger than the music that beats in its heart. In order to understand, for instance, why King Solomon's Mines, the first downtown Minneapolis club to host black musicians and cater to a black clientele, was unfairly raided and closed, we have to understand the levels of corruption and poisonous rhetoric that turned the downtown club scene into a political battlefield. In order to understand why many musicians migrated to the Twin Cities from the South in the late '60s and left disappointed by the early '70s, we have to examine the false promises Minnesota made to minorities in that time period and the destructive decisions that were made by the city and federal government that harmed the African American population in particular. And in order to understand why those scrappy young kids from North Minneapolis were cut off from the rest of the city and led to create their own tight-knit little creative community, we have to study how the construction of I-94, 394, and Olson Memorial Highway razed black-owned clubs and effectively quarantined the black population into small, easily controllable areas.

As I write this now, I am embarrassed to say that while some things have improved, there are persistent issues affecting citizens of color in the Twin Cities that seem the same, if not worse, than they were in the 1960s. I watched with a lump in my throat as Black Lives Matter activists overtook I-94 during protests in 2016 in response to the brutal and unjustified police shooting of a St. Paul elementary school employee, Philando Castile. It wasn't just that their passion and commitment to their cause were enough to stop traffic; the protest was powerful because the young activists were literally walking in their elders' footsteps, reclaiming ownership of the historic black neighborhoods that were lost to the freeway's construction. When they shut down the stretch of I-94 between Dale and Lexington, the protesters were literally screaming, singing, and marching their way through the heart of the long-lost Rondo neighborhood.

And when protestors sat in the freezing cold and rain for eighteen days in November 2015 in front of the Fourth Precinct police station in North Minneapolis to protest the city's response to the shooting of another young black man, Jamar Clark, it was impossible to ignore that the precinct sits on the exact site of the defunct North Minneapolis community center named The Way, which was once regarded as a safe haven for aimless youth and politically minded young activists who needed a space to breathe and plan, when they were embroiled in similar conflicts in the late 1960s, and which served as an incubator and a launchpad for many of the artists we now associate with the Minneapolis Sound.

Music can be an incredible lens through which to view our world. It can unite us in times of loneliness and isolation, and it can heal us in times of struggle. It can teach us profound things about ourselves and our relationships, and it can help us to express the things we thought were unspeakable.

* * *

Volumes have already been written about the Minneapolis Sound's impact on the larger pop world, from Prince's reign over the 1980s to Jimmy Jam and Terry Lewis's continuing success as producers for top-selling artists like Janet Jackson. Which is why you'll note that the narrative arc of this book concludes with Prince's debut in the First Avenue Mainroom on March 9, 1981; it was the first time Prince crossed over to the more mainstream white rock audience in his hometown, and the moment when many tastemakers and historians say they knew the Artist was about to launch into the stratosphere. The incubation of his sound was complete, and he was ready to take it global.

Where my interest lies is in examining that sound, turning it around, taking it apart, and studying it from the inside out. What is the Minneapolis Sound? Do you know it when you hear it? Is it when synthesizers replaced the traditional horn parts present in funk and soul music, updating the genre for a generation who grew up watching the moon landing and became obsessed with *Star Wars, E.T.*, and contemplating life in outer space? Is it found in the fact that funk, rock, new wave, and dance music had never been combined so potently? Or is it in the fashion, the sexual expression, the pure celebration of togetherness and funked-up freedom?

To start at the Sound's explosion in the early 1980s and move backwards, digging deeper into where it all started, exposes an intricate and winding root system of different genres and scenes. There are the more obvious lineages—like the bustling jazz community that inspired a new generation of artists to pick up horns and write parts for their friends' soul bands, or the gospel music that taught teenage bands to harmonize their voices over the chug and churn of the more secular rhythm and blues. Tracing those roots brought me all the way back to 1958 (coincidentally, the year that Prince was born), which was when the first R&B band from Minnesota was captured on record.

And then there are the curveballs, like the fact that black artists had an added incentive to stay up to date on all the Top 40 hits by popular white artists of the day so they could get gigs playing for the Twin Cities' predominantly white audiences, especially in the 1970s, when the hard lines around "black" and "white" musical genres had started to erode and iconic artists like Jimi Hendrix and Carlos Santana were reinventing what it meant to be a minority musician making popular music. Or that young African Americans could barely access music being made by progressive black artists on Twin Cities airwaves, with the only early black-oriented community radio station, KUXL, barely audible outside a one-mile radius of its North Minneapolis-adjacent station.

So it's no surprise that musicians from the area were especially prone to melting different sounds together, infusing their work with a scintillating blend of jazz, soul, R&B, funk, disco, early punk, new wave, dance, and all different kinds of rock 'n' roll, from Sun Records to psychedelia, country-rock to prog. But the sound goes so much deeper than labels; it is also defined by a relentless drive and demand for excellence. You can hear it even in the earliest recordings: a pulsing, indefatigable energy, as if every musician who participated in the development of the sound were on a quest to take first place in a competition whose final score could never be tallied. It was an unrelenting desire for Black Excellence, for a slice of that hometown pride, for the loudest applause, for respect. And it propelled artists from every genre, every neighborhood, and every ethnicity to come together to create sounds that were leaps and bounds ahead of their time.

Researching this book was simultaneously wrenching and inspiring, eye-opening and heart-rending. It was a process that relied heavily on the oral histories of the people who experienced these movements, and their willingness to share their stories with me. After spending countless hours speaking with musicians about their memories, driving around with them through the neighborhoods where they came up, and combing through the newspaper archives of various Minneapolis and St. Paul libraries, I learned things about the city that I will never unsee; I sat in awe contemplating the perseverance that was required to create this music and organize these shows. Even when confronted with utter hatred, bigotry, and ugliness, the music persisted, and the artists' quality of work remained undisputed. Even when their clubs were repeatedly closed and they were forced back underground time and time again, they never stopped singing. A sense of urgency and hope remained.

It's also impossible to welcome you into this narrative without noting the monumental losses to the Minnesota music community that we endured in the three years I was researching this book. Obviously, Prince's death on April 21, 2016, sent a shockwave across the entire globe, and I never could have imagined that I would finish writing this book in a world that didn't have him in it. It was the honor of a lifetime to speak with him directly about some of the topics that are included in this book, and my only hope with this work, as with anything I write about him, is that I do the man proud. Thank you, sweet Prince. You made me a better writer in ways I don't know that I'll ever be able to explain, and your legacy will forever be interwoven into the city I call home.

Minneapolis also suffered the loss of the tremendous saxophone player Morris Wilson, whose 1979 album *Fantasy Island* will live forever as the most underappreciated experimental jazz-funk album to come out of Minnesota. (Seriously: cop that.) In addition to being a fiercely talented player and composer, Morris was also a huge advocate for the promotion of black music in the Twin Cities.

And speaking of advocates, it was heartbreaking to learn of the passing of Minnesota's pioneering home studio engineer, Gaity Records' David Hersk, who recorded the first 45 by an R&B band in the state (by the Big M's); Dean Constantine, who ran King Solomon's Mines in the face of significant adversity; and James Martin, who managed two of the most popular St. Paul R&B vocal groups of the early 1960s, the Amazers and the Exciters. Finally, as the book neared its publishing date, we learned of the devastating loss of the soul singer Sonny Knight, who was in the midst of a glorious second act of his career.

Learning of these losses during the research of this book only added to my urgency in getting it all down on paper. While this book is far from a comprehensive guide to every musician who had a hand in shaping the Minneapolis Sound, I hope it brings us a step closer to better honoring and documenting the unsung men and women who poured their lives into this music.

The title of this book is borrowed from a wonderful song from the Lewis Connection's 1979 self-titled album. Not only does the song perfectly illustrate the cross-pollinating collaborative nature of the R&B and funk scene of the late '70s: also, the song is billed as the Lewis Connection but was actually recorded by the Family, with lead vocals by Family frontman Sonny Thompson, playing by the Connection's Pierre and André Lewis, and a little guitar work and background vocals by a young Prince Rogers Nelson, who was something of an understudy to the older generation of players. Given the narrative arc of the book, the sentiment of the lyrics feels profound.

Of all of the songs I'd listened to and sentiments that I'd heard expressed in interviews and articles, it was this lyrical passage that stood out. In one succinct phrase, Sonny Thompson—who Prince would later recruit to play in his New Power Generation and give the stage name Sonny T.—captured the eternal search for a sense of belonging amid chaos and discord, the reclamation of what is "ours" versus what is "theirs," and the overwhelming sense of place that came to define this era and sound: "There's got to be something here for us."

Chapter One

•

PLYMOUTH AVENUE

LONG BEFORE it would be occupied by protesters, before urban renewal and highway construction would raze its historic buildings, and before the riots of the late 1960s burned several shops to the ground, Plymouth Avenue was simply the bustling street that served as the central corridor of the Near North neighborhood of Minneapolis. Lined with Jewish-owned grocery stores, delis, appliance showrooms, banks, and record stores, Plymouth Avenue was the gathering space for the area's largest Jewish population and its small but growing African American community. The neighborhood had long been known as a magnet for immigrant populations, thanks to its affordable housing and proximity to downtown, and by the early 1960s the population was shifting again, welcoming an influx of young black men and women who had moved from the South in search of better-paying jobs and a more welcoming place to live.

On a sunny day in 1960, Plymouth Avenue was simply the place where a seventeen-year-old Willie Walker could go to wash his dirty laundry. Walker was new to town and doing his best to mind his own business, sorting clothes at the laundromat off Plymouth and Seventh Street, when a teenager named Timothy Eason strolled up to him and looked him up and down.

"You really do look like you can sing," Eason said.

Looking east down a bustling Plymouth Avenue in the late 1960s. The street was lined with Jewish-owned shops and cafés. Photograph by Mike Zerby. Copyright 1968 Star Tribune.

"How do you look like that?" Walker asked.

"Well, can you?" he pressed.

"Yeah," Walker replied. "Can you?"

Soon, they were "washing our clothes and singing harmonies in the laundromat," Walker remembers, laughing. "He left the laundromat and went up to the corner and got another couple friends and came back, and we started a group that same day."

Walker had moved up to Minneapolis from Memphis and was already a seasoned musician, having sung in his hometown park with friends from the time he was eleven years old, and in a professional gospel group, the Redemption Harmonizers, starting at age fifteen. The gospel group had given him a chance to start working the church circuit, first in the South and eventually up to Minneapolis, and he liked the city so much that he decided to pack his bags and move to the Twin Cities.

"We came to Minnesota three times in '59, and after the second time I told them it wouldn't be a good idea to go back to Minnesota, because I liked the place," he remembers. "I said if we go back to Minnesota, I'm gonna stay."

Walker's experience mirrored that of many of the young African American musicians who would relocate to Minneapolis and St. Paul in the early 1960s. The young soul singer Sonny Knight relocated from Mississippi to Minneapolis in 1955, the same year that gospel artist (and eventual manager for Minneapolis vocal groups the Exciters and the Amazers) James Martin moved from South Carolina. The trailblazing R&B artist Maurice McKinnies, who got his start touring the South as a guitarist for the blues artist Big Maybelle when he was just sixteen, migrated from Florida to Minneapolis with his family in 1960. And by 1963, the Twin Cities were attracting higher-profile talent: the Memphis-reared harmonica ace Mojo Buford, who was already an established player in the Chicago blues scene, came to Minneapolis in 1963 to form the R&B-leaning Chi 4.

In hindsight, the growth of the minority population in Minnesota seemed quite small compared with national trends; according to the U.S. Census Bureau, the statewide population of persons of color in 1960 was hovering at 1.2 percent in Minnesota, compared with 11.4 percent of the total population of the United States. But since most African American families were clustered in a few specific geographic areas, their increasing presence was noticeable. The high schools in the city's most racially diverse neighborhoods (North High School in Near North Minneapolis, Central High School in the heart of South Minneapolis, and the Mechanic Arts High in Rondo, St. Paul) saw obvious changes in the demographics of their classes between the mid-1950s and early 1960s, and the African American students who were musically inclined started gravitating toward one another and forming a tight-knit yet competitive little scene.

It wasn't the first time that an exciting underground scene had been developed by black artists in Minnesota. Years before these

The Ebony Club, seen here in 1957, was one of several clubs on Sixth Avenue (now Olson Memorial Highway) to host early jazz and R&B shows in the 1940s and '50s. City of Minneapolis photograph. Courtesy of Hennepin County Library.

young players moved to town, and years before R&B music was even invented, a different kind of swinging sound was coursing through the streets of the North Side and Rondo. Starting as early as the Prohibition era of the 1920s, another busy thoroughfare in the Near North neighborhood, Sixth Avenue (later named Olson Memorial Highway), was home to a stretch of underground hangouts that hosted the birth of jazz in the Twin Cities, like the Blue Note and Old Southern Barbecue, and earlier spots like the Clef Club Cafe, Boulevard, Rum Boogie Cafe, and Cotton Club.

"In the Twin Cities during Prohibition, speakeasies, after-hours joints, and 'private' clubs serving liquor and playing jazz opened their doors and blossomed," Jay Goetting wrote in his book *Joined at the Hip: A History of Jazz in the Twin Cities.* Much like a dizzying scene from an F. Scott Fitzgerald story, these late-night clubs were home to a woozy, loose, and swinging set where gangsters and ne'er-do-wells mingled shoulder to shoulder with the hippest music lovers, business owners, and local celebrities in town.

When Prohibition was lifted in 1933 and liquor started to flow aboveground once again downtown, the majority of the musicians who performed in these underground haunts got gigs playing up and down Hennepin Avenue at strip clubs and cabarets. But for the black musicians who cut their teeth on Olson Memorial, there were no jobs to be found downtown.

"I don't know what caused it, but there was nobody working. You'd go up and down Hennepin, and you wouldn't see any black faces entertaining," remembers pioneering saxophonist Irv Williams, one of the first black players in the area to break the color barrier and perform with a white band. So the speakeasies and after-hours hangouts persevered, providing a necessary place for black artists to mingle with their white peers and for musicians of all backgrounds and ethnicities to explore more adventurous sounds. "They were officially illegal, because they had gambling and sold liquor after hours," Robert Alan Stebbins wrote in a 1960s thesis called "The Jazz Community: The Sociology of a Musical Sub-Culture" about the venues along Olson Memorial. "They were extremely important to the jazz life of the town, because they provided an opportunity to musicians to play the kind of music they liked."

It was in these off-the-grid spaces where many of the state's pioneering jazz artists shared stages with touring acts of the time like Duke Ellington and Count Basie, who both participated in an after-hours jam session for the ages at the Boulevard when they were passing through town in 1944. "Things usually started swinging at the Boulevard about one or two in the morning," wrote journalist Jim Bennett in a 1964 article called "Jazz in the Twin Cities." "There was always action while you waited for the bands to show up [after] their gigs in the big ballrooms downtown. From ten-thirty on, musicians drifted in one or two at a time and found chairs near the front of the room. By midnight the little bandstand couldn't begin to hold them all. The musicians were blowing from their seats around the dance floor, and some from little tables on raised platforms that lined the walls of the room. . . . You ordered beer and watched the crowd, and if you felt like it, you sat in for a set on drums, or piano, or bass, or whatever horn you'd brought with you."

On the surface, thanks in large part to the majority Jewish population that had settled in the area and opened businesses along Plymouth and Olson Memorial, the Near North neighborhood

Musicians gather and wait their turn to play during a jam session at the Blue Note while organist Billy Holloman and saxophonist Jimmy Wallace perform. Photograph by Charles Chamblis. Courtesy of the Minnesota Historical Society.

appeared to passersby to be a predominantly white, buttoned-up place. But vibrating just underneath the surface was an exciting culture of cutting-edge music and black nightlife. As the next generation of young black musicians came of age in North Minneapolis, the allure of these underground spaces was downright intoxicating.

"This church that I grew up in was kitty-corner from the Blue Note; the Blue Note was on Eleventh and Lyndale in North Minneapolis. And I used to stand outside church and look across the street at the Blue Note while my mother would be talking to me, and the church members were yanking on my arm. Doors opened, the sound of the jukebox—that was always pretty cool to me," recalls Maurice Jacox, who would go on to play saxophone and flute in one of the Cities' first interracial R&B bands, Willie and the Bumblebees. As soon as he was able, Jacox started hanging out at the Blue Note, soaking up the knowledge and energy of his elders in the community.

"Every musician, every jazz musician of a certain age, every black musician got their start at the Blue Note," he says. "I wanted to be a real player, so I was going over to the Blue Note, and players would invite you up on stage. I had two songs, playing on flute. They let me come up and play my two damn songs on flute. Every player was a good player. You got to be a good player because real players encouraged [you] and gave [you] a chance and gave access to some of the knowledge that you need. It's the tradition of music, to help the next generation. So that's kind of what happened with me and a lot of other players—got their start playing way over their head at the Blue Note."

"When I was in the tenth grade, I used to go over there and sit in, with Billy Holloman and all them," says Pierre Lewis of the Lewis Connection and the Family. "It was like a real small hole-in-the-wall, and I don't know how they did it, but they would fit a hundred people in there. Every Monday they had Blue Monday. It was a raggedy hole-in-the-wall, but boy, there was some good music coming out of that place."

* * *

After his harmony-filled singing experience at the laundromat with Timothy Eason, seventeen-year-old Willie Walker became fast friends and singing partners with Eason and his crew. That same day, Eason went down the street to the corner record store to fetch his pals Jimmy Crittenden and Joe Dibiaso, and by nightfall they had officially started a group that they would name the Valdons. Not long after forming, they crossed paths with an up-and-coming concert promoter in the neighborhood, Dick Shapiro, who would soon become a dominant force in the live music world. And before they knew it, they had gained a following and become one of the first secular black vocal groups to gain traction in Minnesota.

As was common at the time in North Minneapolis, the Valdons' first audiences were primarily Jewish youth—teens celebrating bar mitzvahs, birthdays, and graduations at the local synagogues and dance halls. "[Shapiro] knew what he was doing, because the jobs paid us well for that time. We did a lot of synagogues. At the time that we were starting, [he] was starting his Central Booking Agency, so we were his first project," Walker says. "He was of Jewish descent and he was well connected with the community, and he was actually providing 99 percent of the entertainment for whatever they had going on."

Like many teenagers in the late 1950s and early '60s, the Valdons and their fans were gravitating away from the jazz and big band sounds that their parents loved and toward a style of music that was more emotional, vocally driven, and direct. And for kids raised on church music, adapting their voices to fit into tight gospel-influenced harmonies seemed only natural. "We were playing the Isley Brothers—a lot of Isley Brothers. The Drifters, Platters, the stuff of that nature," Walker remembers.

A peek at the *Billboard* R&B charts in 1961 offers a glimpse at the popular music of the time: the Miracles' "Shop Around," Ben E. King's "Stand By Me," and Ray Charles's "Hit the Road, Jack" illustrate the popularity of rollicking, shuffling, rhythm and blues–inspired pop songs. It was also a crossover moment for the gospel genre; when the Isley Brothers' "Shout!" premiered in 1959, church groups pushed back against the song because they felt the merging of gospel with rock 'n' roll felt downright blasphemous—a sure sign that a new youth movement was under way.

Although records by these artists were charting nationally in the early 1960s, it was harder for teens in Minneapolis to get their hands on many songs by black artists. The Twin Cities has historically been a majority white-focused radio market, and it was especially uncommon in that era to hear popular black music coming across the airwaves. So kids in North Minneapolis soaked up most of their musical knowledge from the record store on Plymouth Avenue and their television sets, taking notes on the hip swivels of Elvis Presley and the sharp matching suits of the Isley Brothers and the Temptations.

In fact, it was television first and foremost where Sonny Knight recalls being exposed to modern music. "You look at Elvis Presley up on television doing what he does, and I guess if music is in you, that's gonna be what you wanna do somehow." Knight started performing around town with a band called the Blue Jays and cut his first record when he was just sixteen years old. Because of his age and his stature, they called him Little Sonny Knight. Much like Willie Walker in the laundromat, Sonny Knight had a surprisingly easy time connecting with other young musicians; from almost the moment he knew he wanted to pursue it, he was introduced to other kids looking to form a band.

"Back in the day you could get these little reel-to-reel recorders for about $20, so my aunt got me one, and I was messin' around with it at home and stuff like that, and I got to singing on it," he remembers. "And then a friend of mine that I went to school with came by and was hanging out in my house, and I was playing it for him and he heard it and said, 'That sounds cool, man. That you singin'?'"

"Yeah, that's me," he replied.

"You can sing!" his friend said. "Hey, man, you oughta come and check out my brother's band."

Knight went down and auditioned for the band, "and then next thing you know I got the job . . . . we started playing little things here and there, and that gave me a little more experience into playing, understanding singing, getting out a little bit more into the music world."

The giddy energy of these early days is palpable in the way the artists retrace their memories. Back in that era, it was incredibly rare for young, grassroots artists to get the chance to go into a studio to record music, so most of the attention was paid to perfecting the live show and learning how to win over a crowd with tight harmonies and slick dance moves. Which makes it hard to pinpoint exactly what the music *sounded* like as this new scene was just starting to form; many of those sounds only exist in the musicians' memories, or in the echoes of the songs that would be recorded later on.

But not all of the sounds were lost to the sands of time. Thankfully, though he didn't even know it at the time, a young Jewish teenager named David Hersk ended up recording a couple of R&B groups from his high school in his makeshift studio in his parents' basement—and one particular recording by the Big M's goes down in history as the first R&B record to ever get cut in Minnesota.

David Hersk grew up at 1501 Newton Avenue in Near North, just two blocks north of the bustling business corridor on Plymouth Avenue. "The North Side was a wonderful neighborhood to grow up in," David recalls. "You could walk anyplace, and you didn't have to worry about anything."

Like so many of the families that had settled in the neighborhood in the midcentury, David Hersk came from a Jewish family, and his experiences studying Hebrew at temple and preparing for his bar mitzvah would open an unlikely door for David into the music recording world. "Believe it or not, the interest in recording was with my Hebrew teacher, Mr. Chirchic. He recorded my bar mitzvah lessons for my thirteenth birthday, which was on a Wilcox-Gay Recordio machine, and I was fascinated by that. I told my parents [that if I had one] I could tape things off the radio." David was a big fan of the radio back then and would spend hours listening to the AM station WDGY to catch the latest from groups like the Drifters and Johnny Ace. He figured if he got his own recording device and bought a stack of blank records from the music shop, it would be cheaper than trying to keep up with buying all the latest singles. His parents bought him a Wilcox-Gay Recordette, which had an arm for playing records

A young David Hersk in his basement studio in the late 1950s. Photograph courtesy of Denny Johnson and Tom Campbell, Minniepaulmusic.com.

R&B band the Teen Kings perform for fellow students at a dance at North High School. Photograph from the 1960 *Polaris* yearbook. Courtesy of the Hennepin County Library Yearbook Collection.

This 1959 single by doo-wop group the Velquins (note the common
misspelling of *Valquins* on the record) was recorded in David Hersk's
basement studio and pressed on his Gaity Records label. Photograph
courtesy of the author.

and another for cutting, and soon David was in business making his
own records of his favorite songs off the radio.

For Hersk, those earliest memories of connecting with the recording process were filled with wonder. "Merle Edwards had a show
on WDGY radio. It was the only teen radio show at the time," he says.
"It was Uncle Merle, and I told him I would like to record. I called in
and said I would like 'Rock around the Clock' with Bill Haley. And I
remember him putting down the radio time, and he mentioned in
his announcements, 'I'm going to hold this for young David Hersk
to start his recording machine so he could get the whole thing.' So
that was my first real recording."

Before long, David's classmates at North High School were asking him to record songs off the radio for them, too, and he had set
up a workshop in his basement to launch his first business capturing

The Velquins were one of the Twin Cities' first doo-wop groups, along with the Wisdoms, to record for David Hersk's Gaity Records label in 1959.

bootleg radio recordings for his classmates. One thing led to another, and by the time he was entering his junior year in 1955, David had earned enough money to build a makeshift recording studio in his basement where his classmates' bands could set up and play. His parents helped him finish out the space with an acoustic tile ceiling and paneled walls, and he created a small control booth with a window where he could oversee the recordings. "I charged five hundred dollars for a thousand pressings and three hours of studio time," he says matter-of-factly. When asked how high schoolers in the '50s were able to come up with that kind of money, he just smiles. "Parents were." Word of mouth spread through North High School and to some of the first rock 'n' roll bands coming out of St. Paul's Central High. Soon David's home recording business was humming.

The Big M's recorded the two songs for this release in David Hersk's basement studio in 1958. The 45s were pressed at Kay Bank and released on the band's own Laura Records. Because so few were pressed, very few copies of this historic 45 still exist; not even David Hersk had a copy at the time of our interview. Photograph courtesy of Derik Olson.

"I also had a job. I worked at United Hardware Distributing—Hardware Hank, as probably everybody knows it. I was working in their advertising department, and my mom was manning the phones, booking appointments for me," he recalls. "I also did a lot of high school bands, as far as their band concerts or choir concerts. I did MacPhail recitals, too."

The albums would come pressed with a logo from David's new label, Gaity Records. To this day, an original pressing from David's label is highly sought after in the collector's market, especially considering how influential many of those primitive rock 'n' roll and R&B bands ended up being. On the rock side, David captured the first recordings of the Glenrays, the String Kings, and the Sonics, all of whom were predecessors to the garage rock explosion that would

Brothers Howard, Walker, and Walter Munson *(left to right)* were founding members of the historic Big M's, the first Minnesota R&B group to cut a 45. Photographs from the 1958, 1962, and 1964 *Polaris* yearbooks. Courtesy of the Hennepin County Library Yearbook Collection.

sweep Minnesota in the early 1960s and put one of David's rivals, Soma Records, on the map.

When reflecting on the recordings he captured in his basement in those tender high school days, David remembers he admired the R&B bands the most. "All these African American groups were terrific," he says. "We became good friends. We went out to lunch together. We went out to Embers or we went out to Porky's. When I recorded the Wisdoms and the Velquins—the doo-wop groups—I wish I would have known the people at Motown, like I knew them later on, to license them."

Looking over his catalog of recordings, David picks out three R&B–leaning groups in particular that he wished he could have elevated to the national stage: the Wisdoms, the Velquins, and the Big M's, a supergroup of sorts that comprised musicians who would go on to shape the sound of black music in the Twin Cities for the next two decades.

Listening to the recordings of the Big M's all these years later, it's easy to see why David Hersk was so impressed. A pair of songs captured by David and pressed on Kay Bank's Laura Records offers the first taste of the sounds that were emanating from the North Side. On the 45's A-side, "Silent Lover," the recording is scratchy and the different band members' contributions seem to bleed into one other to create a blur of soulful sound. You can practically envision the band hauling their guitars, basses, drums, and saxophones down into David's basement and cramming into his studio to cut the song to wax. The song swings, with a vibrant saxophone part chugging underneath a sparkling vocal melody, and the rhythm section works the beat so nimbly that you can practically visualize the thread extending from the Big M's all the way to the hard-driving funky and gritty R&B bands that would dominate the scene a decade later.

The B-side, "Get Going," is equally enchanting. The piano-driven backbone of the song keeps it firmly rooted in the teen-bop and pop sounds of the era, but the band's enthusiasm and energy is audible; this was a band that was just getting started, and chomping at the bit to show the city what they could do.

The Big M's band was anchored by a group of brothers who were raised in Near North neighborhood and attended North High School with David Hersk: Walker, Walter, Howard, Buddy, and Lamar Munson; the revered singer Charles McKinney; the saxophonist Morris Wilson, who would influence the R&B and jazz scene in the Twin Cities for the next several decades; the piano player Sanford Margolis, who would go on to play in the Minneapolis Symphony Orchestra; and toward the end of their reign, the rising R&B star and newbie in town, Maurice McKinnies.

The band went through many different incarnations in the years they played together, cycling in new players as the older members would graduate from high school; with Walker Munson leading the group, over time he would hire players like the influential guitarist Eddie Lovejoy and the bassist Willie Murphy, who would go on to found the 1970s R&B party band Willie and the Bumblebees. "The Big M's were the really hot North Side black band," recalls Murphy. "That was my schooling, you know. Playing on the North Side."

As for many of the high school bands of their era, opportunities abounded for bands that were willing to schlep their gear around the metro area and play school dances and other social functions. As Lamar remembers it, the Big M's got big enough that they even required a roadie to help them get from place to place. "They used to roll around with their equipment in a big old hearse," Lamar recalls, chuckling. "They often did what you'd call a battle of the bands—they would play onstage together back to back. Because at that time they would give dances and then they'd say it's a battle of the bands, so they'd have the Big M's and then the Jazz Knights or the Teen Kings or someone like that playing."

Lamar was the youngest of the Munson brothers to be enlisted in the Big M's, coming into the group after they had already been established as a formidable live force. He notes that Walker Munson was the first in the group to become a trained musician and start encouraging the younger generation of artists. "My oldest brother Walker, he went to MacPhail in Minneapolis, and he graduated from there with a BA, so he was actually my ninth-grade music teacher at Lincoln Junior High School in North Minneapolis," Lamar says. "And he did a lot of things in the community with music, and he helped a lot of kids." This is fascinating, especially given the long legacy of music education and mentorship that would become a defining characteristic of the Twin Cities soul community. Almost as soon as the R&B scene became a sensation in Minneapolis, members were already reaching a hand down to the younger and less-experienced players to pull them upward toward excellence.

The Big M's established a practice that would continue throughout the next several decades of fluctuations and musical evolutions in the local scene: they hired players from all different backgrounds, not for any political or social reasons but because North Minneapolis was still relatively integrated in the 1950s, especially in the classrooms, and they were a product of their surrounding community. "They had black guys, they had white guys. There were only a few Latino guys in the Twin Cities, but they also had a couple of those [players]. They were very diverse. And they had Jewish people—because you couldn't go to Minneapolis North, and Lincoln, and not [work] with Jewish people," Lamar recalls.

In addition to going down in history as the first Minnesotan R&B act to record a 45, the Big M's were also honored as the second act to be inducted into the Minnesota Rock and Country Hall of Fame.

Not long after the Big M's visited David Hersk's basement studio, two more doo-wop groups would descend the stairs at 1501 Newton: the

The Wisdoms perform on KSTP's *Hi Five* program, backed by the rock 'n' roll band the Flames.

Velquins and the Wisdoms. Unlike the Big M's, whose band included bass, drums, and guitar, the Velquins and the Wisdoms operated as a capella vocal groups. Inspired by Frankie Lymon and the Teenagers and their runaway hit "Why Do Fools Fall in Love," teenage vocalists throughout the city were eager to create their own harmonic pop hits, sometimes only accompanied by a spare piano backbone and the snap of their own fingers on the two and four beats.

The Wisdoms, which included St. Paul Central High School students Jerry Reed, Horace Rivers, Ray Brown, and Gene Moore, earned a quick following throughout the city of Minneapolis for their quick-footed dance moves and tender harmonies. In July 1959, a year after forming, they would record a pair of songs, "Two Hearts Make One Love" and "Lost in Dreams," and release their 45 on Gaity Records. The A-side is as sweet as can be, a romantic doo-wop ditty about a protagonist's undying love for his dear. The B-side hints at something a little more aggressive and rock-oriented, with members of the white garage rock band the Flames stepping in to add a marching-drum shuffle beat and a tiny sprinkling of surf-oriented guitar work.

It was also in 1959 that the Wisdoms and the Flames would be invited to appear on KSTP's *Hi Five* program, which was modeled after Dick Clark's *American Bandstand*. Although they'd never experienced any discrimination at their live shows, despite playing parties in several different neighborhoods, it was at one of these televised events that the Wisdoms first experienced how impenetrable Minnesota's racial barrier was in the 1950s. "We were good dancers and girls wanted to dance with us," Gene Moore told Jim Oldsberg's *Lost and Found*. "Predictably, a white girl would ask one of the Wisdoms to dance. The station, however, didn't condone interracial dancing."

"Because of our popularity, we were confident that Rob Hubbard, the owner of KSTP, wouldn't deny us the opportunity for singing programs altogether," added Horace Rivers. "Our group had a brazen unwillingness, however, to compromise on who it was we could dance with, but our confidence was tempered with a healthy dose of reality. . . . Unlike Elvis Presley, who could only be shown on TV moving from the waist up, the Wisdoms could only be shown dancing on television from the waist down."

The same Central High School hotbed of musical talent would also produce the Velquins, who recorded their songs "My Dear" and "Falling Star" with David Hersk in 1959 and would perform with the backing band the Teen Kings. Both sides of the record sound more closely intertwined with the popular doo-wop of the day than the Wisdoms' harmonic soliloquies, calling to mind hits by the Platters.

Because these burgeoning groups had to travel across the Mississippi River to North Minneapolis to record their 45s with David Hersk, the early recordings from the Velquins and the Wisdoms provide the first links between the Minneapolis and St. Paul soul scenes that would strengthen over time. Unfortunately, the very thing that would soon make it easier for young musicians to get back and forth between the two cities—the construction of Interstate 94—would also have a dramatic impact on the growing African American music communities in Minneapolis and St. Paul.

Chapter Two

•

RONDO

Every freeway is a political statement.
—LEWIS MUMFORD, *The Highway and the City,* 1968

ERMAN JONES GREW UP in the heart of St. Paul's historic Rondo neighborhood at the height of its vibrancy. Looking back on it now, he speaks about his neighbors and his memories with a bittersweet tenderness, and a reverent sense of awe. "If I could just take you back there," Herman says, letting out a gentle laugh, his eyes softening. "If you lived in St. Paul, Rondo just popped," he continues. "I'd walk out of my house and walk down the block, and there was Rondo: everything you could think of was right there. The pool hall, the BBQ places, after-hour places, anything you needed. Everything was right there."

To listen to Herman Jones talk about his childhood is to conjure black-and-white images of an idyllic and bustling community, with local shop owners waiting around the corner to meet every need and friends traveling through the streets in tight-knit circles. Older folks would pass the time sitting on front porches, keeping an eye on the passersby, while the younger generation of moms and dads would dress in their finest clothes and head out on "the strip" to see live music and go dancing. "The whole neighborhood was just full

Women in elegant cocktail dresses line up to dance at a social club in Rondo in the 1950s. Photograph by Earl McGee. Courtesy of the Minnesota Historical Society.

of music," he remembers. And from an early age, he soaked up that music and excitement as much as he could:

> My dad and my mom, they would go out and it was a whole family thing—my auntie, the sisters, they all went out in a bunch. So they'd all come up to the house, since we lived right around the corner from Rondo, so we would all meet at the house about six o'clock; the house is poppin'. They'd have a party at the house, and

all the kids would be there, the cousins and everybody, and they would leave us all there at the house and start walking down the street and around the corner, everything was right there. And I remember we would stay up there on the weekend until one, two, three in the morning, until they got home, and then the next morning, the aunts and the uncles and my mom would all be cooking breakfast. After breakfast, lunch, and dinner, we'd all be out in the streets playing. And you really knew your cousins; you knew your family. And everything was tight-knit. Family was everything.

Like many of the historic black neighborhoods that had grown in prominence throughout the country in the 1940s, Rondo was small and self-contained; there was no real reason for African American residents to have to leave the borders of their neighborhood, which Herman Jones and others described as a small town within the bigger city of St. Paul. Much like the Near North neighborhood that was centered on Plymouth Avenue and Olson Memorial Highway, Rondo the neighborhood was anchored at Rondo the street, which stretched from Lexington Parkway to Western Avenue, a distance of about two miles.

"I remember as a kid, before the freeway came in, you'd walk down the hill and walk up, and everything was just right there. It was like a little bowl," Herman remembers. Although most of Minnesota is relatively flat, geographically speaking, Rondo had its own peaks and valleys, and the earth seemed to bow down around this place, as if cradling it in its hands. It's easy to see how such a shape could reinforce a sense of unity; it was easy to stand on the side of the hill and survey it, scanning from block to block, the perfect rows of houses providing an all-American backdrop for the pulsating energy of a creatively restless underground scene.

But those sloping hills would eventually work against the people of Rondo. As residents of the Twin Cities are well aware, those valleys that twist and turn toward the State Capitol and downtown St. Paul no longer contain houses. That's the path cut by one of our state's busiest highways, I-94, which shuttles millions of people between

Minneapolis and St. Paul every day. If not for the residents of Rondo who so proudly repeat their stories, pressing their memories into history like handprints in the concrete of those bulging highway overpasses, the incredible legacy of this creative, charismatic, and loving black community would be all but erased.

It's a story that Herman Jones saw coming from a mile away—literally. He remembers when the Highway Department came knocking door to door, offering to buy up all the houses, and how his dad, John, got hired to work on the construction crew assigned to build the big new freeway that would connect the two sides of the river. Herman was just old enough to finally start playing in the music clubs himself, like the Western Lounge, but when his dad's crew started working on the stretch of highway at Franklin and Riverside, just over the Mississippi in Minneapolis, and moved slowly eastward, there was a foreboding sense that all of these hotspots and nightclubs might not be long for this world. Soon it might all be gone.

To fully appreciate the story of Rondo, the neighborhood that St. Paul wiped away, we have to start further back. We have to go back to those early memories Herman had about watching his parents get ready to go out on the town, and the dreams that lived in all these young kids who were wondering what these dance halls and nightclubs were all about. We have to go back to the beginning. And in the beginning there was so much music.

Much like with what was happening in North Minneapolis and other black, urban neighborhoods around the country, the popular music of the 1940s was jazz: big band music, military-style marches, Dixieland, and in the years following WWII, a more improvisational form of bebop popularized by Dizzy Gillespie and Thelonious Monk. This was the kind of music that the people of Rondo might go out and experience on a Saturday night, first cramming into the tiny barbecue joint Booker T's to listen to it on the jukebox, flooding the dance floors at social clubs up and down Rondo like the Sterling Club, Cameos, and Zodiacs, and staying up late listening to records at after-hours spots sprinkled throughout the neighborhood.

In those days it was common to catch the Pettiford brothers, Oscar and Ira, working their way through the club circuit in both

The Booker T. Cafe and Tavern in 1960. This was a favorite spot for eating ribs and listening to the latest jazz and doo-wop on the jukebox—and one of many Rondo businesses lost to the construction of I-94. Photograph by the *St. Paul Dispatch and Pioneer Press.* Courtesy of the Minnesota Historical Society.

Minneapolis and St. Paul. Due to Oscar's stature in the larger national jazz community—he is considered one of the founders of the bebop genre and performed with everyone from Duke Ellington and Dizzy to Miles Davis and Monk—the big-name performers of the era would drop by these so-called jive joints to jam with the local talent when they passed through town.

Rondo was first established as a neighborhood in the late 1800s, and by the 1940s it had become a vibrant and recognized African American neighborhood. The population of Rondo was roughly 31 percent black in the 1940 census, and as more and more African Americans migrated to the capital city from the South, they would gravitate toward Rondo. By 1960, one census tract in the Rondo area was registering as high as 65 percent black.

As the minority population grew, the divides between white and black areas of the city deepened. The crowds that gathered at these small Rondo clubs, houses, and restaurants were predominantly black, and it provided folks with a space safe to gather and build community, shielded from the harsh effects of discrimination and prejudice that were pervasive in other areas of the city. "A person could be a shoeshine man during the day, but he could be Mr. President at night," Marvin "Roger" Anderson noted in an oral history for the Minnesota Historical Society, reflecting on his father's participation in the Sterling Club on Dale and Rondo.

As the years progressed, the popular jazz music of the day gave way to the blues, and kids who came of age in the early 1950s like Marvin and his friend Floyd Smaller Jr. recall singing along to singles like Hank Ballard and the Midnighters' "Annie Had a Baby" with other teenagers at "jumps," or house parties they would throw at each other's houses when their parents weren't home. Smaller, Anderson, and their friends from the Elks marching band had their own social club, the Crazy Eight, that would hop around the block in matching suit coats, ties, and jeans, dropping into neighborhood parties and singing for their friends. "We used to try to sing, but it wasn't anything too official," Anderson said.

"We were pretty popular," Smaller said in another Minnesota Historical Society oral history. "The parties where we'd really go would be the parties the older folks had, and we were some of the young people that was not invited, but they knew we were always going to crash, so they kind of left the door open for us to show up. And if we didn't, they were a little disappointed. We'd go in and dance with all the old ladies and everything. We'd have a ball."

By the time Herman Jones and his peers were old enough to start their own bands, the time was right for a group of teenagers from Rondo to come together around a new style of music—one that combined the hard-driving, jumping basslines of rhythm and blues with the smooth melodies of doo-wop and the hair-raising wails and stacked harmonies of gospel. Even in its earliest forms all those years ago, the first traces of the Minneapolis Sound were created by combining different genres of black music to create something new. "That gospel–R&B–funk sound came, and that was really the sound of Minnesota," Herman says. He ended up having a front-row seat to the birth of this new sound, as both a member of the Exciters and

A promotional photo for The Amazers, featuring *(left to right)* Napoleon Crayton, John Price, Billy Barnes, Bill Lordan, Charles Singleton, and Joe Moore. Courtesy of Bill Lordan.

as a musician who often went head to head with the Exciters' main rival, the Amazers.

Herman traces this all back to a band manager named James Martin, who moved to Rondo from South Carolina in 1955 and was already heavily entrenched in the touring gospel circuit before starting to manage more secular, rollicking R&B bands. Martin was only seventeen, but he quickly learned the lay of the land, meeting other like-minded people and figuring out how to book shows and connect musicians with recording equipment and engineers. When the gospel group the Mighty Golden Voices moved to St. Paul from Texas, Martin fell in with their group. And when they changed their name and started dabbling in R&B, they asked him to be their manager. Led by the young phenom Napoleon Crayton—still regarded to this day by his peers as one of the most naturally gifted singers and songwriters of the era—the new group called themselves the Amazers. And almost immediately upon rebranding, they began to live up to that name. "The Amazers were kind of the lead. They was kinda the number-one group in the Twin Cities," Martin recalls.

They had the moves. They had the matching suits and slicked-forward pompadours. And they had the songs—not just covers of vocal and R&B hits of the day, like so many of their contemporaries would sing, but original tunes penned by Crayton that tugged at the heartstrings and sent the harmonies scrambling for the rafters. In fact, they were one of the first bands of their generation to mix original tunes into their set lists and capture them in the studio, thanks to the sharp melodic skills of Crayton. His showstopping, harmony-laden ballad "It's You for Me" was first captured and pressed by the historic Kay Bank Studios, home of hits by the Trashmen and the Castaways, and released by the local Bangar label.

The band's talent was so evident that they were soon recruited by Curtis Mayfield to open for him on his tour with the Impressions and record a 45 for his label, Thomas. To this day, some of the only audio evidence that exists of the Amazers are the two songs on that 45, which was released in 1967. The A-side is a cover of "Without a Warning" by the Controllers' Lenny Brown, but it's on the B-side, a clearer capture of Crayton's "It's You for Me," that the appeal of the Amazers is most obvious. The love song floats along on a Temptations-invoking pop chord progression before splitting open into a chorus that reaches for the heavens. By the end, all three singers—Crayton, Billy Barnes, and Jonathan Price—are screaming their way through the melody like their throats are on fire. Just imagining the group performing it live at one of the tiny clubs in Rondo is enough to send goosebumps up both arms.

Herman Jones remembers vividly one show his band the Exciters played with the Amazers. It ended up being a night that the Impressions came to the Twin Cities to play the Marigold Ballroom, and two young bands from Rondo were tapped to open the show. "These guys [in the Amazers] had these different colored suits: one had a pink suit, one had a white suit, one had a blue suit, one had a yellow suit, with shoes to match. Bass player, drums, keyboard, guitar, and Napoleon sang while he played keyboard, and he had two other singers, Billy and John. The place was packed. All these ladies were just going crazy. The song 'It's You for Me' was playing on the radio, and they looked like a million bucks.

"We went on before the Amazers; we opened. We got to play

The Amazers recorded this 45, which featured the Napoleon Crayton original "It's You for Me," for Curtis Mayfield's Thomas Records label in 1967. Courtesy of the author.

maybe about half an hour, forty minutes. Then these guys came on and they were really the show; they were the headline. The Impressions had no idea and had never seen or heard a group like that, ever. Those guys got done, and it was like the Impressions weren't even there. They had to come on after. They weren't prepared at all. We were watching them, and we looked over and the Impressions were standing there, with everyone screaming and the lights on. I remember the bass player, Jimmy, saying, 'Man, I feel sorry for the other guys. I feel real sorry for them.'"

"I remember feeling goosebumps when I heard the singers do a high-pitched squall, which is a controlled scream," remembers Bill Lordan, who played drums in several Twin Cities soul groups, including the Amazers. Lordan would go on to perform in Sly and the Family Stone and the Robin Trower band, touring the world many times over, and he still holds his time spent with the Amazers in high esteem. "The Amazers' gospel roots would influence my entire career," he remarked. "Gospel music is the root of soul music, for sure."

With the Amazers leading the charge, there would soon be other acts that would combine their gospel roots with more contemporary soul influences and start competing for stage time. Which brings us back to Herman Jones, whose story began in those nascent early days of Rondo's musical history. Back in the early 1960s, Herman Jones was still a teenager at the Mechanic Arts High School in St. Paul, a school that would be hailed as a melting pot for the growing number of minorities living in Rondo and the city's East Side. He was a budding drummer, who just happened to live across the street from a musician who was only a year ahead of him at MAHS, the guitarist and keyboardist Leroy Hawkins, and he was already starting to make a name for himself in the band the Gladiators. "Everybody had a little group or a little name, like the Turquoise, and you know, everybody started in a garage or on somebody's front porch, and as you got better, you started meeting new guys," Herman recalls.

Herman and Leroy were already early fans of the Amazers, and James Martin saw the potential of creating more bands in a similar aesthetic. Since James was friends with Herman's dad, he soon tapped Herman to join Leroy and the cousins Jimmy and Arthur Williams to form a new group that would go by the name the Exciters. "The whole idea was, we were hoping [to play with] the Amazers and be on the same show as them, but we had to grow, so he had to make some changes," Herman remembers. It was the early 1960s and the band was barely out of junior high, still figuring out how to interact with each other onstage. But Martin had found a secret weapon: Wee Willie Walker, who was already tearing up the North Side of Minneapolis as a member of the Valdons.

"He put Willie Walker in there, and Willie was older and he was an experienced singer. Then he had three or four other singers that were gospel, and they were switching over, so we were going to be a band of nine men," Herman says, recalling that the initial hope was to showcase a quartet of vocalists with a backing band, à la the Temptations. "But because Willie wouldn't really want to sing with the four singers, he wanted to do that solo act: when the smoke cleared, it was Willie Walker and the Exciters. . . . Willie was kinda like the older guy. He took care of us. He was that older guy that you looked up to, and we were his boys. That's what he used to call us: 'My boys.'"

Herman remembers rehearsing for hours at James Martin's house, then getting shuttled from bar to bar for gigs long before he was of drinking age. "My dad and mom were really supportive 'cause I was a good kid. I was responsible, and my dad, he would put me in the car and he would go along. I was doing something other than running the streets like so many of the other boys, so he would put me and Leroy in the car, and he would take us to parties and he'd drop us off, come back and pick us up. We played at the Western Lounge and Booker T's, those kind of places, and he'd be right there. Sometimes my mom would come, and the whole family, all my aunts and uncles, they would all be there."

The Exciters found their footing as an agile backing band, which would work in their favor. For the majority of the 1960s they became a go-to support band for rising young singers, first for Wee Willie Walker and later Jackie Harris and Professor McKinney, among others, and Herman Jones would keep the band going in various incarnations well into the 1970s. But their time being a strictly Rondo band was limited to those few years in the early '60s, before Rondo itself would be turned inside out.

The Federal-Aid Highway Act was passed in 1956, channeling massive amounts of federal funding into major cities across America to jump-start the construction of our national freeway system. But it's important to note that the planning for interstate construction in Minneapolis and St. Paul had started long before the funding was secured from the federal government. Starting as early as 1920, city engineers drafted plans for various highway routes, and by 1938, a federal interstate map traced a path for I-94 that would connect Chicago, Illinois; Madison, Wisconsin; the Twin Cities; and Fargo, North Dakota. As soon as I-94 was a possibility, the path it would make as it cut through Minneapolis and St. Paul was up for debate, with two

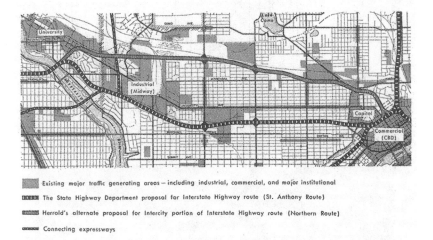

Existing major traffic generating areas — including industrial, commercial, and major institutional

The State Highway Department proposal for Interstate Highway route (St. Anthony Route)

Herrold's alternate proposal for Intercity portion of Interstate Highway route (Northern Route)

Connecting expressways

The two proposed routes considered for the Minneapolis–St. Paul stretch of I-94. From Alan A. Altshuler, *The City Planning Process* (1965).

routes strongly considered: the "St. Anthony Route," which would bend slightly south as it approached St. Paul, cut through Rondo along St. Anthony Avenue, and curve northward toward the State Capitol; or a less popular route, the "Northern Route," that had been proposed by the St. Paul city engineer George Herrold, which would arc northward and run adjacent to railroad tracks north of St. Anthony Avenue.

"By 1945, St. Paul's eighty-two-year-old 'founder of city planning' George Herrold, considered in local political circles to be an 'unbending idealist,' was voicing what he considered to be significant concerns about the use of Saint Anthony Avenue. Using the proposed route would decimate the long established Prospect Park and Rondo neighborhoods, essentially cutting the life out of them," writes historian Matt Reicher. But Herrold was outnumbered, and his idea was never seriously considered by the city. In 1947, the St. Anthony Avenue plan was approved by the St. Paul City Council.

It should be noted that as these discussions were taking place, not a single resident of the Rondo neighborhood was included in

I-94 construction crews dig up dirt in Rondo between Grotto Street and St. Albans Street, while a row of residential homes on St. Anthony Avenue remains untouched just beyond the roadwork. Courtesy of the Minnesota Historical Society.

the dialogue. In fact, years would pass before residents would have a chance to voice their own concerns about the Minnesota Highway Department's plans. "Leaders of the African American community became aware of the approval of the St. Anthony route in 1953, six years after it occurred. It came up because there was a push to rehabilitate a school in the affected area, and it was learned that the school was in the path of the proposed freeway," the researcher Patricia Cavanaugh writes in a report on the Twin Cities Interstate System. Several community organizations sprang up in response to freeway construction, including the Rondo–St. Anthony Improvement Association, which formed in 1955. But community leaders were disadvantaged in both their timing and political power; as soon as the Federal-Aid Highway Act passed, the Minnesota Highway Department was ready to swing into action.

The effects of the highway's construction were felt deeply by those in Rondo, and the statistics of I-94's aftermath are staggering. "One in eight African Americans in St. Paul lost a home to I-94. Many black-owned businesses, such as barbershops and movie theaters, were lost and never replaced. Of the homes demolished, 72 percent had been homes to African Americans. Research conducted after the relocation found that the density of non-white residents increased in all parts of the surrounding non-white area. What formerly had been a vibrant mixed community became primarily black and economically depressed," Cavanaugh concludes. Or, in the words of Tom Lewis in his blazing analysis of the cultural and racial impacts of the interstate system, *Divided Highways*:

> In building the Interstate Highway System, we displayed ourselves in all our glory and our meanness; all our vision and our shortsightedness. We showed democracy's virtues and not a few of its vices. The highways represent the height of American technological achievement; but no one, not the engineers, the planners, the builders, not even the naysayers—those who opposed the highways—understood how the roads would ripple through the culture.

Another musician who clearly remembered the music community in Rondo is Sonny Knight, who came to St. Paul from Mississippi in 1955. Sonny had a unique take on the way the neighborhood shifted in the '60s, because like so many young men his age, he was drafted for the Vietnam War in 1965, and he didn't end up back in Minnesota until 1969.

In the final few years of his life, it was common to see Sonny howling his way through song after song onstage at First Avenue's Mainroom, or in front of a sea of fans dancing while the sun goes down and the midway lights come up at the Minnesota State Fair. Sonny was one of many artists from the literal old school of soul who enjoyed a resurgence in the 2010s, nearly fifty years after their first bands were formed and their first albums recorded. To watch

Sonny Knight, photographed in 2014 as he began a new act in his career with his band the Lakers, preparing to release his breakout album *I'm Still Here*. Photograph by Nate Ryan. Courtesy of the photographer.

Sonny Knight performing in his glorious, long-awaited second act was to see the millennial generation's delayed yet energetic embrace of classic soul play out in real time; he performed backed by seven or eight young white guys, all in their twenties and thirties, who weren't even born in time to see Prince explode onto the scene, or to catch a glimpse of the generation of predecessors who were getting their hands around this purple sound.

I met up with Sonny on a warm spring day in 2015 following the release of his big sold-out release show at First Avenue for his comeback album, titled *I'm Still Here*. Sitting on a park bench in the Milwaukee Avenue Historic District in South Minneapolis, Sonny looked at the rows of perfectly manicured and preserved houses that were built in the 1880s for low-income workers. By all accounts, the Milwaukee Avenue houses shouldn't even be here anymore; by the end of World War II, most had fallen into such bad disrepair that they were nearly torn down. But thanks to a preservation project in the 1970s, they were rehabilitated and added to the National Register of Historic Places. The fact that Sonny chose this peaceful, perfectly preserved location to talk about the decimation of Rondo is almost too poetic to bear.

"I like it here. It takes me back in time," he says. "It feels good—these things have been here as long as I've been here. If only these houses could talk."

Back in the '60s, Sonny and his peers were a long way from playing a room like First Avenue. With few paying club gigs to speak of, the black R&B and soul musicians of the era were often relegated to playing what many of them refer to as the "chitlin' circuit": "It's like what's left of the hog," Sonny explains. "It's not the big ham or the bacon or anything like that. It's the chitlins, the lower class, in the bowels of everything. Those were the kind of places that we were playing."

Bands ended up entertaining for a scraped-together scene of rented dance halls, VFWs, hotel ballrooms, back rooms, and basements that could accommodate the bands and their audiences when no mainstream businesses would. The Nacirema Club in South Minneapolis. The Cozy Bar in the Near North. The Peacock Lounge in the Warehouse District. Dirty Girty's in St. Paul. Despite the growing popularity of soul and R&B music, these were the only rooms that would host bands with all or mostly black members, even as the civil rights movement surged nationwide, even in liberal Minnesota.

When Sonny first started gigging around Rondo as a teenager, he remembers playing VFW halls and community centers. When he returned from the war in 1969, everything had changed; most of his old neighborhood had been destroyed. "They tear down everything that has anything. They took out a lot of good businesses, and people kind of scattered. They're still scattering way out to suburbia," Sonny says. "The mom-and-pop variety stores, drugstores, different things like that—they're all gone to the new modern convenience of one drugstore to serve them all."

The interior of the Cozy Bar, one of few underground spaces available for black R&B bands in the 1960s. Courtesy of Jimmy Fuller Jr., whose father, James Fuller Sr., owned the Cozy Bar and later the Riverview Supper Club.

Likewise, the corner bars and houses that once hosted intimate dance parties have been traded in for more above-board and more closely monitored venues closer to the center of the city. The construction of I-94 through Rondo had a devastating effect, not just on the houses and businesses that lined the blocks but on also some of the few black spaces that had been created for the purpose of experiencing and celebrating live music. By 1968, when traffic opened on the stretch of I-94 that joins the Mississippi River to downtown St. Paul, Booker T's and the Western Lounge were all but a fading memory. The interstate was yet another force that seemed designed to keep black music underground.

Chapter Three

•

THE WAY

I see no more dangerous development than the build-up of
central cities surrounded by white suburbs.
—MARTIN LUTHER KING JR. to students at the University of
Minnesota, April 27, 1967

S O MUCH OF OUR SHARED CULTURAL HISTORY is fluid; a specific event might lead a person to shift their feelings or pivot
their life in a different direction, but it's not always easy to
pinpoint where one movement begins and another leaves off. In
music history, especially, the edges seem to blur around who inspired
whom and what specific events led to the creation of new and in-
novative sounds. But if you trace the histories of the musicians who
are chiefly credited with the creation of the Minneapolis Sound—
Prince, Morris Day, André Cymone, Jimmy Jam, Terry Lewis—a pattern starts to emerge. Before they made it big, all of these big names
spent some time in their formative teenage years jamming in the
back room of the community center on Plymouth Avenue, The Way.

In order to understand why this space was not just vital but necessary for the young kids of Prince's generation, it's important to
take a few steps back and examine the events that unfolded in North
Minneapolis in 1966 and 1967 that would forever alter the social

The Way, pictured here in 1975 after it was rebranded as "The New Way." The building sat at the corner of Plymouth and Morgan Avenues in Minneapolis. Courtesy of the Minnesota Historical Society.

fabric of this neighborhood. In one of the most truthful and autobiographical songs of his career, "The Sacrifice of Victor" from 1992, Prince sang about the unrest that plagued his neighborhood when he was a young boy:

> Dr. King was killed and the streets
> They started burnin'
> When the smoke was cleared, their high was gone
> Education got important, so important

It wasn't just a flight of fancy that he dreamed up for dramatic effect. When Prince sang about the streets of North Minneapolis burning, he was recalling very real events from his youth that are still being unpacked today. Much like the I-94 construction that dismantled the once-vibrant Rondo community, North Minneapolis would endure its own series of challenges in the 1960s that would reverberate throughout the next several decades and change the neighborhood forever.

Despite the fact that the black population in the Twin Cities had started increasing—the Census Bureau reported that it rose from 1 percent in 1950 to four percent by 1965—the average black citizen was rendered invisible in day-to-day city life due to increasing segregation, white flight to the suburbs, and urban renewal. Like the Rondo neighborhood, the Near North neighborhood of Minneapolis was sliced in half by the construction of the Olson Memorial Highway, which heavily impacted the economic viability of many of the area's corner stores and businesses and robbed it of its cozy, neighborhood feel.

One community member who witnessed this transition firsthand is W. Harry Davis, a boxing-coach-turned-civil-rights-leader who was the founding chief executive of the Minneapolis Urban Coalition. Davis was born on the North Side but moved to South Minneapolis in the mid-1950s to buy a larger, more affordable home for his growing family. He still remained heavily involved with the Near North neighborhood, however, and it gave him a unique perspective from which to observe the fluctuations of the area. "Sixth Avenue was renamed Olson Memorial Highway, after the late Governor Floyd B. Olson, a neighborhood native son. The street was widened and a parkway added down the middle, which had the effect of clearing out the businesses on the south side of the street," Davis wrote in his autobiography. "The project was popular because it provided jobs and eliminated some trashy businesses. But it made my neighborhood's main street a thoroughfare where pedestrians were no longer comfortable and retail business could no longer thrive. That changed forever the character and livability of the neighborhood."

With the expansion of Olson Memorial into an actual highway and excitement about the construction of I-94 and other freeways dominating newspaper headlines, the Near North neighborhood was increasingly being viewed like a thoroughfare and an afterthought, an area you might pass through on your way from St. Louis Park or Golden Valley into downtown Minneapolis. At the same time that the African American population grew in North Minneapolis, the

Jewish immigrant population that once dominated the area started to trickle outward toward the more prosperous neighboring suburb of St. Louis Park. Although Jewish people faced discrimination in the 1950s and '60s, they were able to gain a footing much faster than the struggling black population, who faced the steepest disparities in employment and housing. According to the 1960 census, the median income of nonwhites in Minneapolis was $4,598, two-thirds that of whites.

As the gap between the haves and the have-nots widened, the tension between Jewish and black residents on the North Side was palpable. "Within the span of a few years, shop owners went from being neighbors to semi-strangers who lived someplace else. As the Jewish population assimilated into the larger society, they increasingly became just white folks in the eyes of young black people," Davis wrote. "For a small but increasingly frustrated and impatient share of the black population that remained on the North Side, the shops became a near-at-hand symbol of what white people had and they did not."

Tensions first boiled over on the hot, sticky night of August 3, 1966. It's a date that often gets mixed up in people's memories with further incidents that unraveled the neighborhood in the summer of 1967 and plagued the Selby–Dale area of St. Paul in 1968, not to mention the countless racially charged riots and uprisings that were sweeping through other cities across the nation. Each time the dissonance swelled, the media would proclaim it another "long, hot summer," sensationalizing the discontent. This particular summer evening was long and it was hot, but on that August night in 1966, national events were the furthest thing from people's minds. The Near North neighborhood was just wrapping up a community block party known as the North Side Picnic, and Plymouth Avenue was lined with bored teenagers and twentysomethings who, with nowhere else to go and nothing much to do, used the city's street corners as their gathering spots.

Stories from this evening vary, but Syl Davis, an active member of the Near North community who happened to be working at the social work agency Wells Memorial that evening, witnessed the events and recounted the following in detail for The Way's newsletter:

A group of Black youths returning early from the park had taken up their usual positions of vigilance on the corner of Knox and Plymouth—standing, sitting, discussing the events of the day, the remembrances of the past, and hopes for tomorrow—a usual event that happens wherever brothers can congregate—spectators at a slowly fast-moving passing world.

Another group (8-10 years old) of children on the South Side of the street ran eagerly into the small neighborhood store, there to spend their wealth almost unnoticed by their older brothers. When out of the store they exploded—running, yelling, and the storekeeper right behind them with broom handle (or stick) in hand shouting in a language we all know.

Almost as suddenly, the older brothers were on their feet going over to find out what was the cause of this sudden explosion. They were stopping the younger kids asking them, "What happened?" "What's wrong?" "What's the matter?"

Some of them moved over toward the storekeeper asking him what had happened as he stood just outside his store yelling at them. They demanded, "Hey, man, what's the matter with you? What do you think you're doing? You old—"

Shortly after this confrontation, a relative calm returned when more youths came up and began to talk with the first group. The police came; some stood guard at the store on Plymouth and Knox, others cruised up and down Plymouth. The young people, seeing this, began to tease the police that had come to guard the store. Some began to sit on the ground next to the squad car; others leaned against it. They began to take exception to the statements of one of the officers, and some began to rock the back of the squad car. The officer left—a brick was thrown, then another, and another; then a loud crash from the store across the street. And very suddenly Plymouth Avenue was alive.

The corner store in question was Silver's Food Market, 1711 Plymouth Avenue, and it was damaged along with other nearby businesses, including Koval's Furniture and Appliance.

Peering back at this moment in Minneapolis history through the telescope of time, this event on Plymouth Avenue in 1966 is intriguing for a few reasons. First, the response by the police was starkly different from how they might respond to a similar situation in the post-2000s, or even how they would respond a year later, in 1967, to a similar conflict. On that hot August night, rather than escalating the tension with a confrontation, the police blocked off the street and then backed off, giving the youth the time and space to cool down. Furthermore, the city responded to the unrest instantaneously. By the next morning, meetings were being arranged among the mayor, the governor of Minnesota, the police, community leaders in Near North, and some of the wealthiest and most influential movers and shakers in Minneapolis.

It was clear that North Minneapolis was in crisis, and the city and state's leadership was prepared to swing into action. But at a meeting the morning after the unrest that was convened by Minneapolis Mayor Art Naftalin, Syl Davis looked around the room of thirty to forty adults and noticed a glaring omission: none of the youth who had participated in the previous night's uprising was in the room. "The question came why? How come? What do they want? No one could truly answer, for no one there really knew, not even me. There were no young people present at all," Davis wrote.

Syl went back to the North Side that day and convinced some of the youth to come back to the mayor's office with him. "They spoke about the lack of facilities, parks, playgrounds, recreational equipment, jobs, etc., as part of the problem," Davis wrote. Davis helped the youth convince the mayor to hold an open meeting on the North Side in Oak Park, and at 5:00 p.m. that evening the whole neighborhood turned out. "The meeting was well attended by youth, young adults, old, Black, and White—many spoke and voiced their complaints about recreation, education, employment, welfare, street maintenance, and other areas. . . . It was promised that jobs would be made available within 24 hours."

It was all hands on deck. After the open meeting, an owner of a building on the corner of Logan and Plymouth Avenue opened up his space for the youth to congregate, and as Davis remembers, a few community members "borrowed a record player and some pop was given, so five hundred youth tried to dance inside without much success." Across town that evening—still less than twenty-four hours after the unrest swept Plymouth Avenue—Mayor Naftalin returned to his chambers and started making a list of city agencies and influential business owners who could help out in this trying time. The next day, Naftalin held a meeting at his office with the city's most influential leaders.

"Within 20 minutes, 64 jobs were possible. By 6:00 p.m. that evening, 300 jobs were available," Davis wrote. "The Youth Opportunity Center and the Minnesota State Employment Service were instructed to assist in the processing of these jobs. Later that day we were offered a building at 1913 Plymouth Avenue that read 'Fishing Unlimited,' which was much larger and had some offices, for two months free. The roof leaked [and] the windows were broken in spots, but [it was] better than before. We had no money, no office equipment, nothing; many people came to volunteer in those early days. Many of us stayed up during the time from August 2 until August 9—24 hours, trying to help wherever we could." The building with the Fishing Unlimited sign at 1913 Plymouth Avenue didn't yet have a new name, much less a telephone or other equipment for volunteers to use, but they had a space and a purpose. Jobs were pouring in, the youth were being connected with opportunities, and the Near North community suddenly had a place where black youth could congregate, strategize, support one another, and celebrate without judgment or fear.

In that first week, volunteers threw dances at 1913 Plymouth every night. During the day, a whopping 235 young people were connected with jobs. A ping-pong table was acquired, along with other recreational equipment. When the utilities company came to set up the phone lines for the center, the worker asked what name he should put in the phone book. "The young men looked at each other. It was the first time the idea had ever been talked about," remembers Reverend Rolland Robinson, one of the center's earliest supporters. "They began throwing names out when one of them said, 'Let's call it *The Way*.' Nods of approval went about the circle. They knew it was the right name for the right place and the right time."

The Way had come alive, and a sense of hope coursed through

the Near North Side. But the struggles faced by the growing African American youth population were far from over.

Conversations continued well into 1967 about the root of the unrest in North Minneapolis, and The Way wasn't the only attempt to create a new community center for North Side youth. But it was the first of its kind to be led, staffed, and frequented predominantly by black citizens of the North community. That was intentional: the man who would become the first executive director of The Way, Syl Davis, and his wife, Gwyn Jones-Davis, spearheaded a movement for The Way to become a self-sufficient nonprofit organization, and for its staff to purchase the building and have full control of the property.

All The Way needed was cash. And of all the people to bankroll a fledgling community center for troubled youth in North Minneapolis, a wealthy white oil magnate who owned the tallest building in the city might have been far from everyone's first guess. But Raymond Plank, CEO of Apache Corporation, was just the person The Way needed to help it get off the ground and gain control of its future. Plank, who was starting to dabble in civic outreach, was already in the process of trying to get a chapter of the Boys Club opened in North Minneapolis, but the events of August 1966 added urgency to the endeavor and shifted his understanding of the area.

Plank recounts his experiences with The Way in his autobiography:

> Syl [Davis], his wife, and a group of the ardent African-Americans sat down with me and gave me their pitch. Whereas the Boys Club would be welcome, the time before it became available delayed its usefulness. Further, the Boys Club itself was a "whitey project." They needed and wanted a facility sooner, where the leadership was black, the kids black, and the work getting the building prepared would involve the kids, black volunteers, and otherwise unemployed labor, and, "You, Whitey, need to help us with sponsorship and business community funding."

And produce the funding he did. According to financial records for The Way, Plank helped to raise $24,000 and personally wrote checks totaling $50,000 over the first four months of The Way's operation, making him by far the biggest funder of the center, and a huge reason why the staff of The Way was able to negotiate the purchase of the building at 1913 Plymouth.

"There was a crowded chaos both inside and out," recalled A. Karim Ahmed, in a newsletter that was mailed to supporters of The Way. "The place was swarming with young children and teenagers along with the older staff members and innumerable visitors. The construction workers, the electricians, and the painters were continually pushing people from one room to the next. Everything was makeshift, and to make things worse, there was no plumbing in the building. And yet, amidst this incredible tangle, there was an order about things that could only have come from people who were willing to make the best of the situation."

Dances and social events were held. Equipment was scraped together to assemble a practice space for young musicians, and soon The Way had its first house band, a group of teenagers who simply called themselves the Young Players. In the coming years, another band, The Family, would emerge as one of the city's first genre-blending R&B/funk/rock bands and would nurture some of the most influential players in the Twin Cities, including a young Prince Rogers Nelson.

But in those early days, The Way was simply a group of people from all corners of the community coming together to do something, anything, in the face of a crisis. "An impressive cross-section of individuals, Black and White, rich and poor, prestigious and unsung, came together with common concerns to do something constructive and life-giving," recounted Mahmoud El-Kati, a revered member of the North Minneapolis community and the education director at The Way from 1967 until 1970. "They sought to make a sensitive and intelligent response to the demands of the times, to make common cause in responding to the demands of their community. The collective efforts of these citizens, after much deliberation, focused their efforts on building an institution that would address the most conspicuously unmet needs of the most disorganized segment of the Near North Side Minneapolis community."

People from The Way community center formed a human barricade to keep sightseers from driving down Plymouth Avenue while community members cleaned up the aftermath of the 1967 unrest. According to the *Star Tribune,* "There was a near incident at 2:45 p.m. when three white youths in a maroon Mustang refused to turn at Morgan Av. They stopped at Newton and pointed a pistol at The Way traffic directors." Photograph by Earl Seubert. Copyright 1967 Star Tribune.

In The Way's earliest days, the call to action was clear: the black youth living in the area were profoundly disenfranchised. Police brutality and unfair treatment by the criminal justice system were common complaints, as were the increasing rates of unemployment, uneven access to affordable housing, and deteriorating neighborhood centers. As El-Kati poignantly noted (in archived material), "The debilitating environment of Near North Minneapolis pressed inward on the community's most important resource, young people. Lack of opportunity for upward mobility . . . breeds frustration, stifles imagination creating unfocused hostility . . . . alienation in our society is the source of many of the anti-social tendencies engulfing the young."

Although the city's response to the disturbance in August 1966 was swift, leaders did not dig down deeply enough into the roots of the neighborhood's crises, and so tension and discontent continued to fester. As A. Karim Ahmed astutely wrote in The Way's newsletter, "The city reacted by taking the role of a conciliator; it never consciously assumed its own responsibilities, answered the backlog of grievances, or made amends for its years of quiet and silent neglect."

In the summer of 1967, Near North once again plunged into turmoil. "The Minneapolis Riot That Wasn't," a headline from the *Minneapolis Tribune* declared on July 21, 1967, while a separate *Tribune* article published that same day almost seemed to mock the participants in the unrest, commenting that "they knew their lines from other cities," and downplaying the impact of the events by comparing them to much larger and more violent riots that had ravaged other places. Just a week before the 1967 unrest on Plymouth Avenue, a massive riot took place in Newark, New Jersey, that left twenty-seven people dead, and Detroit would be overcome with rioting a few days after Minneapolis.

But the frustrations from the youth who participated in the unrest came across loud and clear and were printed for the entire metro area to see in the *Minneapolis Tribune*:

"We want Black Power," said a youth. "Write that down."

"We're tired of white folks completely," said another.

"We thought we would show them that we weren't going to take any more of this, that we're not going to be pushed around by the cops," said a third.

On July 19, 1967, the sidewalks lining Fifth Street were filled with citizens of all backgrounds and neighborhoods for Minneapolis's Aquatennial Torchlight Parade. An argument broke out between two black women, and police intervened. Bystanders made claims of excessive force, and rocks were thrown. By 11:30 p.m., the unrest had moved up to Plymouth Avenue and dozens of participants were throwing bottles, bricks, fists, and fury. Molotov cocktails were lobbed at the home of Near North Minneapolis's Jewish city councilman Joe Greenstein, and the Jewish-owned Knox Food Market was engulfed in flames.

The next night was even more intense. All of Plymouth Avenue seemed ablaze with anger, violence, and arson. Silver's Food Market and Country House Market, both Jewish-owned businesses, were burned, in addition to Alderman Greenstein's garage and several other buildings. By the time the National Guard was called in on the morning of July 21, there had been eighteen fires, thirty-six arrests, three shootings, and twenty-four injuries.

"It is painful to realize that during the week of disturbances the Northside resembled a besieged city, with several hundred National Guardsmen patrolling the area like an occupied territory," A. Karim Ahmed wrote in a newsletter about The Way. "The audacity and the seeming nonchalance of some of these soldiers strolling in the middle of the street with rifles over their shoulders, with careless disregard for the feeling of human beings around them, may be indicative of things to come for Minneapolis."

As with the events in 1966, the reaction from the city government came quickly, but this time, both the mayor and Alderman Greenstein seemed overwhelmed by the discontent of the black community. An open meeting was called following the events of July 19–21, and more than six hundred North Side residents attended to express their dismay. "If the mayor and the governor and everybody else don't do something to help the Negro, tear the whole damn North Side down!" one woman shouted.

"I may have failed, but I didn't fail because I didn't believe in humanity and justice," Mayor Naftalin told the crowd, who interrupted his speech many times to voice their outrage. "We're all responsible, every one of us," he said. "Last August apparently we didn't do enough. I'll share the responsibility if you'll extend your hand, and we'll go forward together."

Alderman Greenstein seemed less optimistic. "I don't know where I've failed," he said. As in 1966, many promises were made to the black community following the unrest and community meetings. More meetings were promised, as were additional social services and

Young people attended a street dance at The Way on July 21, 1967, the night after unrest swept Plymouth Avenue. The dance was "chaperoned" by Minnesota National Guardsmen, who carried rifles with fixed bayonets, and the newspapers described the event as "jovial." Photograph by the *Minneapolis Tribune*. Courtesy of the Minnesota Historical Society.

Community members gather for a street dance outside The Way on July 21, 1967. Photograph by Charles Bjorgen. Copyright 1967 Star Tribune.

resources. But the guarantees being made to the minorities and poor on the North Side felt increasingly hollow.

"This year's violence, of July 19 and 20, has reinforced our findings about what happened on August 3, 1966. We have determined that the causes of violence, in both cases, run deep into the problems with which the Negro people, other minority people, and poor whites in our city are living. And we have concluded that there is a direct parallel between the conditions existing in Minneapolis and those in other cities throughout the U.S.," read a report by the Minneapolis City Council's Commission on Human Development in August 1967. The commission, which comprised Raymond Plank, future Minnesota governor Arne Carlson, and future Minneapolis mayor Charles Stenvig, among others, had originally been tasked by Mayor Naftalin to pinpoint the reasons behind the violence of 1966. By the time their report was issued, their findings were even more timely and needed. The report continued:

> Due to the failures of the white majority, portions of the Near North Side have become a wasteland, a dumping-ground for all that is unacceptable to the white community in Minneapolis. The conditions on the Near North Side seem not to have changed, and the discontent of the Negro people has increased. The cries for change have become louder but needed physical and human changes have come too slowly. Plans are on the drawing boards, but most of the Negro people feel that they are about 100 years behind schedule.

As part of their research, the commission interviewed numerous citizens in the Near North community about their discontent. Although the interviews were published anonymously, they still prove to be a unique window into the tenor and timbre of the time. "They sat down there and they talked for months and months and nothing was done," one resident said. "But as soon as a brick was thrown, they started sweeping the streets and collecting the garbage regularly—something they should have been doing all along. And the people see this and they say, 'Well, if I tear up a store, that's how I'm gonna get action.' They can't help but think that violence is the only way to go."

"They're tearin' down those old houses for a freeway, and that's the reason they give for not fixin' any of the others up," another neighbor remarked. "But is that freeway gonna help us? No, Sir. All it will do is cut us off further from the city. They're buildin' it so the white man can whiz by and look at the ghetto without havin' to drive through it."

"We have found a city that has been losing its population since 1950—a city that can no longer maintain its younger and more prosperous families," the commission concluded. "The extent of the flight from the city becomes apparent when we observe the significance of our population figures—those age 65 and over are increasing, the number of people earning under $5,000 a year is increasing, the minority population is on the rise and the number of above-average income families is on the decline. In short, our city is following the same pattern as other cities. The higher income groups are leaving and the poor remain."

While those in power sought to make drastic changes to the landscape of the city, those on the far right saw an opportunity: the national discourse was starting to swing toward more conservative theories, and the fallout from the race riots that were sweeping other cities was making its way back to Minnesota. Even Plank, who had previously received positive recognition for his work with the Boys Club, found himself facing pressures from the white political and business communities. "Riots nationally and disturbances locally have provoked fear and controversy, while bringing into the open the prejudices on both sides of the color line," Plank wrote in an editorial column in the *Minneapolis Tribune* in early 1968. "I have been roundly criticized, along with press and radio, for 'fanning the flames.' . . . The typical reactionary demands respect of property, convention, and custom, while declining to inform himself of the human injustices at the source of the pain."

The far right criticized the liberal Mayor Naftalin's reactions to the violence and the inability of the local police to quell the unrest.

A law-and-order style of politics was beginning to make its way into national and local politics, and campaigns against Mayor Naftalin and Alderman Greenstein started coalescing within days of the Plymouth Avenue fires. Additionally, Naftalin's ongoing support of community-focused programs like The Way became entangled with the politics of fear spreading across the city. The academic B. Joseph Rosh sums up this political transition aptly:

> During the summer of 1966 through his decision not to run for reelection in 1968, Mayor Naftalin ardently supported The Way. If the national narrative had not been shifting towards conservatism, Naftalin's attempt to foster sociopolitical power for black youths in Minneapolis would have more than likely been supported by city government, civil rights' groups and the North Side community at large. Instead such groups, who were fearful of losing their power and influence on the North Side, chose to link Naftalin's actions to the Plymouth Avenue disturbances of July 1967.

Meanwhile, The Way was becoming more radicalized. "You back the colored man into a corner and complain when he comes out fighting," one of The Way's central figures, Harry "Spike" Moss, was quoted as saying in a *Minneapolis Star* article on July 25, 1967. "You wait two or three years while this young generation comes along. They see that if you want anything, you got to take it."

Moss quickly became a leader in a new generation of black youth who identified closely with the larger Black Power movement and gained a reputation for encouraging militancy, especially in the wake of Martin Luther King Jr.'s assassination on April 4, 1968. The media, the mainstream white community, and even elders within the Near North community took issue with some of the more radical elements of The Way, even as the organization was rapidly adding programs to help clean up the streets, educate youth on African American history, and offer young people creative outlets and activities. In a lengthy *Minneapolis Tribune* feature on The Way in December 1968, Patrick O'Brien, a café owner on Plymouth Avenue, referred to the

Harry "Spike" Moss played a prominent role at both The Way and The New Way organizations, beginning as a musical director and eventually taking the helm as director in 1974. He encouraged many of the musical groups who passed through The Way's rehearsal space and was de facto manager of Back to Black, which evolved into The Family. Photograph by Tom Sweeney. Copyright 1977 Star Tribune.

organization as "that crime college" and called it a gathering place for "pimps and prostitutes."

Whether there was any truth to people's nervousness about The Way or not, it contributed to the growing anxiety about the Near North community that skyrocketed following the events of 1966 and 1967. The neighborhood had suddenly shifted from being cloaked in the invisibility of economic depression to being explicitly feared. North Minneapolis was a scary place full of angry people and fire, and it was best to just stay away: "In 1965, there had been about seven or eight vacant buildings on Plymouth Avenue; by April 1968, there were thirty-two boarded-up and vacant buildings," Dick Cunningham wrote in the *Tribune*'s feature on The Way.

The construction that turned Olson Memorial into a thoroughfare was only the first slash through a neighborhood that was destined to be intersected and surrounded by freeways. By the 1970s,

The influential saxophonist Morris Wilson, who mentored
many young R&B, jazz, and funk players throughout his career,
was photographed attending a march in honor of Martin
Luther King Jr. on April 6, 1968, two days after his assassination. Photograph by Mike Zerby, *Minneapolis Tribune.* Courtesy
of the Minnesota Historical Society.

I-94 would dissect North Minneapolis, isolating Near North from
its neighbors to the west; another highway called I-355 that would
have connected North and Northeast Minneapolis was approved
in 1970 and led to the demolishing of thirty-five acres of property
and homes. The project was eventually abandoned, new housing
was built, and funds were reallocated to help build Highway 100 in
St. Louis Park. "For a full mile between the alphabetically ordered

cross-streets of Aldrich and Penn Avenues, there is exactly one pre-1967 building still standing," the *Star Tribune* would later note, looking back on this pivotal time for the neighborhood.

With little in the way of political clout or financial power, Near North seemed unable to protect itself from the rapid deterioration caused by urban renewal and white flight. Though they couldn't stop it, community members and the staff of The Way instantly recognized the impact these freeways would have on their neighborhood. "An invisible wall exists around much of the area north of Olson Highway and west of the river. The wall shuts people into overly crowded neighborhoods which lack the civic amenities provided in other sections of the city. The wall shuts out the larger community's concern for, interest in, and even awareness of North Side problems," the community center stated in its newsletter.

"It all changed that night in early August 1966 when several Jewish establishments were destroyed by fire," Reverend Rolland Robinson reflected in his book about the North Side and The Way. "Within eighteen months the prominent Bethel synagogue on Penn Avenue, just a block from Plymouth Avenue, voted to leave the Near North Side for a suburb known as St. Louis Park; other synagogues would soon follow. By 1968, nearly the entire Jewish community that once flourished in Near North Minneapolis had made its exodus. The riots of 1966 and 1967 made the Near North community, in the public's mind, a Black community."

But even as the neighborhood fluctuated dramatically, The Way would stay its course, providing a safe gathering space for youth in the area to decompress, play, and find work. As the musicians from the North Side R&B community began to set their sights on breaking out of their underground clubs in the growing ghetto and booking gigs in more prestigious clubs in downtown Minneapolis, The Way would remain steadfast, serving as an incubator for the new generation of talent that no one saw coming.

Chapter Four

.

THE MINES

We just kept right on playing.
—HERMAN JONES

THE FOSHAY TOWER rises like an obelisk from the densest thicket of brick buildings in downtown Minneapolis. For decades, it was known as the tallest building not just in Minneapolis but the entire Midwest—our first reach up toward the heavens, and first sign that we were more than a simple milling town.

With the Foshay at our center, Minneapolis was a *city*. We were urban. We were well on the way to becoming a metropolis. And we had the tall building to prove it. Designed as a tribute to the Washington Monument, the art deco style of the Foshay has been an alluring part of the city's urban core since it was built in 1929. The building is now home to one of the swankiest hotels in Minneapolis, the W; back in the 1960s, the Foshay was the place where dentists, lawyers, ad men, and CPAs could rent office space in style, and where restaurateurs could compete to create the most high-class hangout for downtown diners and business clientele.

From the top of the Foshay Tower, you can see fifty miles in every direction, from downtown St. Paul to the airport to the prestigious Carlson Towers in the western suburbs. From the Foshay, everything

The view from the top of the Foshay Tower, looking west toward Near North and the Mississippi River, in 1969. Photograph by Chris Morgan. Reprinted with permission.

looks small and peaceful, a never-ending patchwork of beige buildings and brown riverbanks. North Minneapolis is nestled in the city's shadow, closer than you'd think based on all those years of segregation but also distant—remote.

Standing on the observation deck of the Foshay Tower, it's only natural to reflect on how this beacon of progress heralded a new, modern era for the city. But what's surprising to learn is that the Foshay was also home to another fight for progress: in the late 1960s, it hosted one of the Minneapolis music scene's first big battles for representation and racial equity. As more and more R&B musicians gained fan bases and sought bigger stages for their growing bands, a club on the first floor of that building would go down in history as the first venue to allow black bands to play within the boundaries of downtown Minneapolis.

King Solomon's Mines was opened as a bar and jazz club in the Foshay Tower in the mid-1960s, decked out with crosshatched straw decor straight out of the 1950s film of the same name. In the movie *King Solomon's Mines,* a white damsel in distress played by Deborah Kerr turns an exotic African safari adventure into a dramatic love story. In the club King Solomon's Mines, a white-dance-instructor-turned-bar-owner named Dean Constantine waged a battle against the police and city of Minneapolis to create a space where the city's growing African American population could perform modern R&B music onstage and mingle with white revelers in the crowd.

Though it seemed innocuous at the time, a February 16, 1967, news clipping from the *Hennepin County Review* announcing a new style of music at King Solomon's Mines set the stage for two years of tension:

> King Solomon's Mines, located in the Foshay Tower, has switched from jazz entertainment to a steady diet of rock and roll. Dean Constantine of the club made the decision only recently to try out eleven different bands during this next month. He wants to make it the most swinging club of its kind in the Twin Cities. Last weekend things were indeed swinging with a group called "The Continentals." The dance floor never went begging.
>
> "Maybe in a year," Constantine says, "we may try a one-night-a-week open forum show. We could put microphones throughout the club and introduce controversial guests and topics. It has possibilities."
>
> King Solomon's Mines is open seven nights a week, featuring live music. Constantine just might have the formula.

Within two months of switching to a "rock and roll" format, King Solomon's Mines was showcasing the fiery, sweaty, swooning R&B of the Infinites and the golden harmonies of the Amazers, who became

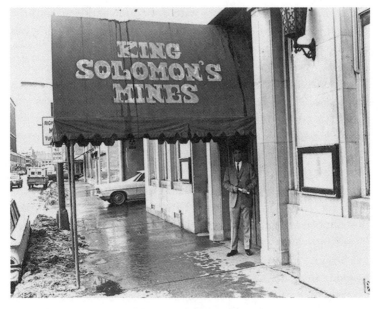

Dean Constantine stands under the awning for King Solomon's Mines, which was located at the base of the Foshay Tower off Ninth Street in downtown Minneapolis. Courtesy of the family of Dean Constantine.

the de facto house band at the club for the rest of 1967. In his weekly column on Twin Cities nightlife, the *Tribune*'s Will Jones described it in May 1967 "as nearly cosmopolitan as we're likely to find in these parts . . . . it's a beautiful, swinging scene."

"I can remember bamboo in different places on the wall, and I guess they tried to make it like a mine, a king's mine," says Wanda Davis, who rose to prominence in the late '60s for her soulful cover of the Aretha Franklin hit "Save Me" and earned the title "Minnesota's Queen of Soul."

"They named it King Solomon's Mines after the movie," remembers Maurice Jacox, a saxophone player best known for his role in the crossover R&B and funk band Willie and the Bumblebees. "They did it up with fake gemstones and treasure chests and African shields on the wall, like some African museum. Shields and spears and pencil spots on things. This mixture with dark and sparkle around the room. It was like you were in a mine or a cave or something. It was really impressive the way they did that."

In his quest to make it the most swinging club in Minneapolis, Dean Constantine was a constant presence at the club, and he oversaw the music and the general vibe of the space. "Dean was gorgeous," Jacox says. "The hair, the suit, oh, the sultry look. Women just went gaga. But he was a fun guy. You realized, he's having as much fun with this as we are. Dean knew lots of black people, and Dean—Jesus, now that I think about it—Dean might have been the first guy in town that actually hired black bands in downtown."

In the years leading up to the heyday of King Solomon's Mines, the number of black bands in Minneapolis and St. Paul had been increasing—but even in the late '60s, any band that had more than one black member had a tough time getting a gig in downtown Minneapolis. In modern-day interviews with musicians from the era, it's a refrain that arises again and again: black bands simply weren't allowed to play for the white audiences that frequented the nightclubs in the urban core. Whether Constantine was aware of it or not, his short-lived club cast the first stones upward at the glass ceiling that hung over black musicians in Minnesota.

Although the musicians performing in bands like the Amazers were far removed from the political activity and fallout that was consuming the Way on the North Side in 1968 (especially since, in the Amazers' case, the musicians were based in Rondo), the unrest that plagued Minneapolis in the late '60s gravitated toward clubs like King Solomon's Mines in unforeseeable ways.

The political pendulum in Minneapolis—and at the national level—had begun to swing dramatically toward the conservative right. Even though the events that took place in North Minneapolis in the summer of 1967 paled in comparison to the full-blown riots that had swept through other cities, the perception of the Black Power movement skewed the way the white majority in the Twin Cities viewed the political actions of the African American minority. The African American population in the metro area was

Dean Constantine stands near the stage at King Solomon's Mines. The décor of the club was inspired by the African safari–themed movie of the same name. Courtesy of the family of Dean Constantine.

still relatively small in the late 1960s. But the ongoing white flight into the suburbs and alienation of the black communities in North Minneapolis and Rondo meant that most white people only saw black faces in the newspapers' coverage of the unrest or television's coverage of the riots happening nationwide, deepening the white population's unfounded fears of blacks, and black men specifically. "There are practically no Negroes," *Harper's Magazine* journalist Fred Powledge noted in a 1969 piece on Minneapolis. "You wonder what the whites are afraid of."

To get a better sense of the white population's attitude toward the black community, the Minneapolis Urban Coalition and the Minnesota Council on Religion and Race teamed up with the *Minneapolis Tribune* to distribute what they called a "Sensitivity Survey" in the fall of 1968. The survey was sent to 238 different Hennepin County churches and synagogues to "tap the prevalence of attitudes, opinions, and beliefs of white churchgoers in respect to the question of race and its influence on the retardation of progress by black members."

The responses were published in the November 18, 1968, issue of the *Minneapolis Tribune*. In response to the statement "I would move into a neighborhood where minority group individuals reside in large numbers," 55.2 percent of those surveyed marked "Disagree." An additional 13.2 percent said they "Strongly Disagree." In response to the statement "I think one must be careful that interracial contacts among teen-agers do not lead to romantic involvements," 40.7 percent marked "Agree," with an additional 11.5 percent marking "Strongly Agree." And regarding the unrest that broke out in the summers of 1966 and 1967, 47.9 percent marked "Agree" and 34.4 percent "Strongly Agree" for the statement "It is as wrong to permit people to starve to death as to burn property."

The conditions were just right for a group of policemen who called themselves the Flying Morals Squad to gain traction in Minneapolis. Led by Officer James O'Meara, the Morals Squad targeted activity that they considered untoward—underage drinking, underground parties, pornography, and prostitution—and were cited in numerous newspaper articles in the late 1960s as "cleaning up" downtown Minneapolis. It was this attitude of targeting "immoral" rather than unlawful behavior that helped to usher in a new candidate for mayor of Minneapolis: a conservative, "law-and-order" police officer with virtually no policy experience named Charles Stenvig.

Stenvig began campaigning for mayor in 1968, following Arthur Naftalin's decision not to run for a fifth term, and his rhetoric resonated deeply with his audience. "Routinely during his mayoral campaigns, Stenvig would raise the specter of Minneapolis's 1967 riots as an example of the real threat of black militancy," write Jeffrey T. Manuel and Andrew Urban in their journal article on Stenvig's rise, "You Can't Legislate the Heart." Stenvig was seen as a straight shooter, proudly anti-intellectual and aggressively authoritarian, who promised to crack down on the crime in Minneapolis—and, perhaps most significantly, to keep it relegated to the neighborhood of

North Minneapolis. "Stenvig imagined the city not as a complex society of various interest groups needing to be effectively managed—this was the vision of liberalism—but as a collection of individuals making moral choices about right and wrong according to conservatively interpreted Christian values," Manuel and Urban argue.

And in the words of Stenvig himself: "My chief advisor is going to be God. . . . And don't you forget it."

Despite the political tension brewing just outside the doors, the music scene blossoming inside King Solomon's Mines was more vivid and exciting than ever. By the summer of 1968, King Solomon's Mines was hopping. "This place would be packed!" remembers Herman Jones of the Exciters. "The Amazers played there, everybody played there."

In addition to house band the Amazers, who went head to head with the Exciters in competition for the best harmony-rich R&B band in the Cities, King Solomon's Mines also hosted one of the city's true crossover acts, the integrated R&B band Dave Brady and the Stars, a group that was led by black vocalists and backed by white players from the rock community. Maurice Jacox jokes that prior to the Mines opening, "once in a while, downtown, you might see a black person by accident." Dean Constantine helped to flip the script in a downtown scene that might have only hosted a black drummer or bass player on its stages every once in a while, Jacox adds. At King Solomon's Mines, all-black or mostly black bands were the norm.

"Dean hired bands like the Amazers, bands like that," Jacox says. "The Amazers had a white guy playing the drums. His name is Bill Lordan. It was an all-black band with a bit of reversal—[I was] trying to explain to black people who this white guy is playing drums, playing all these funky drums. The band, back in those days, all had chemically straightened hair, and Bill chemically straightened his hair like they did. He had the pompadour hairdo and wore the skin-tight Caramelo suits. They dressed in uniforms and Bill looked like the rest of the band, so they got away with it," he says, laughing.

In addition to the Amazers, another popular local act to dominate the Mines was Maurice McKinnies and the Blazers, which

The Amazers rehearse onstage at King Solomon's Mines in October 1967: Toby Zeno (bass), Napoleon Crayton (organ), John Price (vocals), Macray Blackshire (guitar), and Bill Lordan (drums). Courtesy of the family of Dean Constantine.

Vocalist Billy Barnes takes center stage with the Amazers' Toby Zeno *(left)* and Macray Blackshire at King Solomon's Mines, October 1967. Courtesy of the family of Dean Constantine.

would evolve throughout the late 1960s to include more and more members. The singer Gwen Matthews, who would go on to enjoy a decades-long career as a renowned vocalist in the Twin Cities jazz scene, recalls getting involved with the Blazers in 1967, when she was still in high school at Minneapolis's Central High.

"I wasn't supposed to be in these clubs, I was too young," she remembers. "I was headed to college, but then I got an audition and I heard about a band looking for a singer: if you won the contest you'd be the singer, that kind of deal. And I won the contest and started working with the band called Maurice McKinnies and the Blazers. So I worked with that band, with Ronnie Scott playing the organs, Maurice McKinnies obviously was the lead singer on guitar, and this really great guy Donald Breedlove, and Edgar Murphy was playing drums in that band. And then it was me."

The band would gig around town and play at the Cozy Bar and the Blue Note and head out on the road to tour the surrounding five-state area. But it was at King Solomon's Mines where Matthews recalls the wildest shows happened—and where Maurice McKinnies and the Blazers drew their biggest crowds. "We had sellout audiences; most of the time it was standing room only," she remembers. "Especially on the weekends, at King Solomon's Mines, you were in that club, like, you know, if you were at the Fair on one of those circle things that spins around and the bottom falls out? That's how tight it was. I've always described that place like that. I mean, it was crazy."

THIS WEEK!

KING SOLOMON'S MINES

RETURNING TO MPLS.

FOR 14 DAY ENGAGEMENT THE FABULOUS "AMAZERS"

All the latest in rythmn and blues including 'SKATE' & 'BOO-GA-LOO'

Open Sundays & Memorial Day

DANCING 7 NIGHTS

LUNCHES. DINNERS. COCKTAILS

King Solomon's Mines

FOSHAY TOWER—9th ST. SIDE

An advertisement for King Solomon's Mines promotes a fourteen-day engagement by the Amazers. Courtesy of the family of Dean Constantine.

A couple dances close to Gene Williams and the Backsliders at King Solomon's Mines, 1968. Photograph by Mike Zerby, *Minneapolis Tribune*. Courtesy of the Minnesota Historical Society.

In addition to providing a hopping place for the bands to stage their shows, it also became a prime hangout spot for musicians to watch other musicians. Matthews remembers many nights watching the Milwaukee band Harvey Scales and the Seven Sounds tear it up at King Solomon's Mines. "They would come to town and blow up Minnesota. Just blow up Minneapolis. And they were so amazing with their red suits on and their horns. Oh my god, it was crazy," she says.

Pamela Parker, who waitressed at King Solomon's Mines in 1968 while attending classes at the University of Minnesota, recalls how lively and enthralling those live shows could be. "The thing I

Gwen Matthews sings with the Blazers at King Solomon's
Mines, 1968. Photograph by Mike Zerby, *Minneapolis Tribune.*
Courtesy of the Minnesota Historical Society.

remember most is how exciting it was when Harvey Scales came. He
was quite well-known, so he was like a star when he came to town,"
she recalls. Scales had earned a following in the Twin Cities for his
wild stage antics, call-and-response interactions with the crowd, and
pace-quickening rhythm and blues band, the Seven Sounds.

"What I loved was the step dancing," Parker says. "All these guys
in their fancy suits, and Harvey Scales with these different-colored
ruffled shirts—they'd go out on break and come back with a different shirt in another color. And he [had] the Michael Jackson moves
before there was Michael Jackson. He could slide across the floor,

An advertisement for King Solomon's Mines trumpets an appearance by Maurice McKinnies and the Blazers, who performed nightly at the venue in 1968. (Note that McKinnies's name was often misspelled in print.) Courtesy of Secret Stash Records.

and somehow jump down and pick up the microphone in his mouth, and they did some really dirty lyrics to go along with those kinds of things, you know. I loved that."

Despite all of the wild times and excitement happening at King Solomon's Mines, there was trouble on the horizon. In the summer of 1968, race relations and tension over the civil rights movement had heated up to a boiling point. In what is regarded as one of the most historic years in modern U.S. history, the country had suffered through the assassination of Martin Luther King Jr., ensuing riots in more than a hundred cities nationwide, and Robert F. Kennedy's assassination in Los Angeles. The Black Power movement was gaining prominence nationwide, and a single fist held high above one's head had turned from a show of support into an iconic gesture.

Locally, the effects were felt everywhere, from the streets of North Minneapolis to the confines of the most inclusive clubs. Suddenly, everything felt political—even the simple act of gathering for a show. "Yeah, we played King Solomon's Mine on a regular basis," remembers Willie Walker, front man for the Exciters. He adds:

Gene Williams and the Backsliders are caught in a moment of passion while performing at King Solomon's Mines. Photograph by Mike Zerby. Copyright 1967 Star Tribune.

It was a great atmosphere. It was a great job. But it brought about political tension. There were several clubs that were using predominantly black groups, and I guess Minnesota found out that the racial barrier was very strong, because politically, they didn't like the setup with [all] the mixed couples downtown Minneapolis. They didn't like it, so they put their heads together and they closed every place systematically where black musicians were getting work. That made things really rough for a long time.

Walker outlines a belief that is held by many of the African American musicians of his era: that the city of Minneapolis had a specific concern about white women mixing with black men at clubs in downtown, and that there was an unspoken policy enforced until well into the 1970s that targeted bars that booked black musicians within the downtown city limits.

"I've been bucking this thing for ten years," drummer John Arredondo of the Infinites told the *Minneapolis Tribune* in 1969. "I don't know if it's the Police Department or the Council or who, but someone is determined to keep black people out of the Downtown area at night. It's okay for them to go Downtown in the daytime and shop in the department stores. . . . At night though, blacks are supposed to stay in the black bars on the outskirts of Downtown or on the North Side—the Cozy Bar, Peacock Alley, or the Blue Note."

A review of a night at King Solomon's Mines by one of the *Star Tribune*'s most beloved journalists, Jim Klobuchar, illustrates the disconnect that existed between the white establishment and the burgeoning, hip black scene: "My purpose was to get re-oriented to the dances young America is dancing," Klobuchar wrote in a November 1, 1968, column. As he watched a young white woman in a striped minidress do a dance called "the Funky Broadway," Klobuchar wonders in awe that "the joint was fully integrated, the dancers being largely white women and Negro men."

"White men simply cannot do these rhythm-and-blues, bump-and-grind, spontaneous dances," the young woman tells Klobuchar. "They don't have the instincts, timing, or originality for it. And white musicians can't play the music, either. When a white group comes in here the music bombs and the people leave."

In response, Klobuchar writes, "While applauding the Negro's resolute rise in American society, I had to acknowledge these latest attainments do not leave the white honkies much beyond ice hockey, a few mouldering country clubs, and the press agent work for Sammy Davis Jr." This generalized anxiety about black artists' increasing relevance in a largely white world made spaces like King Solomon's Mines more vulnerable to criticism; by the end of 1968, the club had started getting more mainstream attention, and the city's attitude about the space started to shift.

Similar to those early days on the North Side of Minneapolis when after-hours speakeasies and jazz clubs would provide a safe haven for a true mix of humanity, from musicians, athletes, and local celebrities to pimps, hustlers, and street entrepreneurs trying to make the best out of a bad situation, King Solomon's Mines served as a melting pot for the wide range of clientele who weren't welcome at other downtown spots. "The bottom line is, a lot of unsavory characters did hang out there," Pamela Parker recalls. She continues:

> I remember one night we were told to all get behind the bar, and somebody was rushing in—a pimp after somebody, like a girlfriend. But I have to say: there weren't ever any shootings or anything in the bar. Anything that happened that was bad was emanating from parking lots a block away, or across the street. It wasn't coming from inside. Once they got in there, they followed the rules, they did what all the bars do, like set the clocks in such a way so that you have to quit serving plenty of time ahead. Dean was trying to run a straight-up place.

Rather than attempt to kick out or ban certain kinds of folks from frequenting his establishment, Dean Constantine took what some saw as a confusing approach and others saw as revolutionary: he tried to understand them. "I didn't anticipate what poverty and prejudice do to people, but a lot of my clientele were very antisocial," Constantine reflected in an interview with *Insider* in April 1972. "They had chips on their shoulders, and with good reason. White society had done a terrific conditioning job on them. . . . People are always opening up a black club or a white club. I just wanted to open up a human being club. We had policing problems, but do you have to be a karate expert to practice human rights?"

Musicians and staff who worked the club say that most of the scuffles that took place between patrons actually happened out in the parking lot down Ninth Street from the club, which may have attracted the attention of the city more quickly than if they had been indoors. Regardless, only a year and a half into operations, King Solomon's Mines found itself in the bullseye. "The city just didn't want a lot of blacks downtown," Herman Jones says. "And you know, there was a fight all the time. There was a lot of that going on. But at the time, it was within our neighborhood. Now, taking it downtown, it was just kind of unheard of." On August 15, 1968, Constantine was given a list of grievances from Foshay Tower's management, along with a demand that all dancing in the Mines cease. "His lease had not specifically mentioned dancing," *Insider* reported later. "Eventually the management denied him storage, office space, garbage pickup, and a key to his own back door," even though his lease ran through 1971.

Still, the music persevered. King Solomon's Mines wasn't just the best place to see R&B music in the city—it was literally the only place in downtown Minneapolis catering to black audiences. In hindsight, members of the music community speculated that this is why King Solomon's Mines drew so much unwanted attention: the Mines opened its doors to every range of clientele, from players for the Vikings and high-class black businessmen to some of the more troubled souls from the North Side. "The club was a complete spectrum of black urban society from hustlers to insurance agents," *Insider* reported. As Human Rights Commissioner Conrad Balfour would later argue, "One club had to take on the whole darn city. . . . there was only one place to go. . . . So some people were carrying dope, numerically, some people were carrying weapons. And there were also the businessmen. Everybody came down to Dean's place."

The crackdown came swiftly—although the police insisted it wasn't a crackdown.

It was a typical Wednesday night at King Solomon's Mines— swinging, as Dean might say, and packed with patrons. One of the most popular touring acts to play the club, Harvey Scales and the Seven Sounds, was well into their performance, laying down deep funk grooves and asking the crowd to shout back in call-and-response melodies. Suddenly, police descended on the club, locking all the doors and demanding to see everyone's identification. Here is what the *Minneapolis Tribune* printed about the raid:

POLICE HOLD 10 IN RAID TO FIND DRINKING MINORS

OCTOBER 17, 1968

Minneapolis Morals and Flying Squad officers, led by Moral Squad Supervisor James O'Meara, raided the King Solomon's Mines, at 144 S. 9th St., in search of underage drinkers Wednesday night. Ten suspects were held.

Most of the suspects, five females and five males, said they were 21 when booked in City Jail for investigation, according to arresting officers. But Morals Squad officers said most had no identification or false identifications.

O'Meara said the raid might serve as a warning to clubs catering to young crowds that these type of complaints (the squad had received complaints of underage drinkers at the club) will be handled as they were tonight.

"This is no crackdown, but there just might be another raid next week and the following week."

Flying Squad officers sealed off the front door while Morals Officers went through the crowd—which was listening to Seven Sounds, a band from Milwaukee, Wis.—checking identification cards.

Dean Constantine, owner of the club, said he had "bent over backwards to screen out the under-21s. I think we do a better job of screening than other clubs in town. We've turned away hundreds and hundreds who haven't had IDs."

Even though many of the "minors" who were taken to the police station were found to be of age, there was now a permanent black mark on the club's reputation with the city, and what had managed to remain a fairly underground space was splashed all over the town's papers.

Shortly after the raid, the chairman of the City Council Licenses Committee, Jens Christensen, brought his complaints against King Solomon's Mines to the City Council and moved to have its liquor license revoked. On October 25, 1968, Constantine was served with a notice: "You will please take notice that at a meeting of the Licenses Committee of the Minneapolis City Council . . . on November 6, 1968 at 9:00 a.m., the Committee will consider why your license to do business at above establishment should not be revoked by reason of selling liquor to minors and bad character of establishment in general."

But Dean Constantine was not going down without a fight. He rallied his troops, passing a petition around the club and asking his patrons to sign—and to everyone's surprise, signatures on the petition kept coming and coming, filling more than twenty pages, including Earsell Mackbee from the Minnesota Vikings, musicians Maurice McKinnies, Willie Walker, Stephen Crowe, Bill Lordan, and Napoleon Crayton, and hundreds of other supporters: "We, the undersigned, feel that the closing of King Solomon's Mines would be detrimental to the cause of human rights. We hope that the problems with the City Council and the Police Department can be worked out so that King Solomon's Mines may remain open."

Many of the musicians and patrons also attended a City Council meeting to support Constantine. In addition to Christensen's motion to revoke the liquor license for the Mines, Constantine was also met with heavy scrutiny from the Morals Squad and other members of the police. "Police License Inspector Harvey Everson told the Committee this bar has a history of problems and complaints in and near 114 So. 9th St., which is patronized by both black and white persons who come to dance and listen to rhythm and 'blues' music," read the minutes for the November 6 meeting. Everson referred to King Solomon's Mines as "the worst run bar in Minneapolis," and Officer James O'Meara characterized Dean Constantine as "the most uncooperative owner of any establishment he has ever checked," despite reports from several other police officers that Constantine "was very cooperative with them at all times."

Both Everson and Christensen seemed perturbed by the recent raid for underage drinking but also spoke generally about the character of the bar, zeroing in on the kind of music that was being performed and insinuating that there was a connection between the genre of music and the bar's troubles. "Alderman Christensen stated that at the time Mr. Constantine approached his office for approval of the transfer of ownership at this location; discussion arose as the type of dancing to be conducted here," the minutes continue. "The applicant indicated it was not his intent to have the so-called type of 'go-go-blues' operation. However, in listening to the conversation here today, it is very apparent the licensee does, in fact, operate a rhythm and blues–type of dance operation; scuffles and breaking

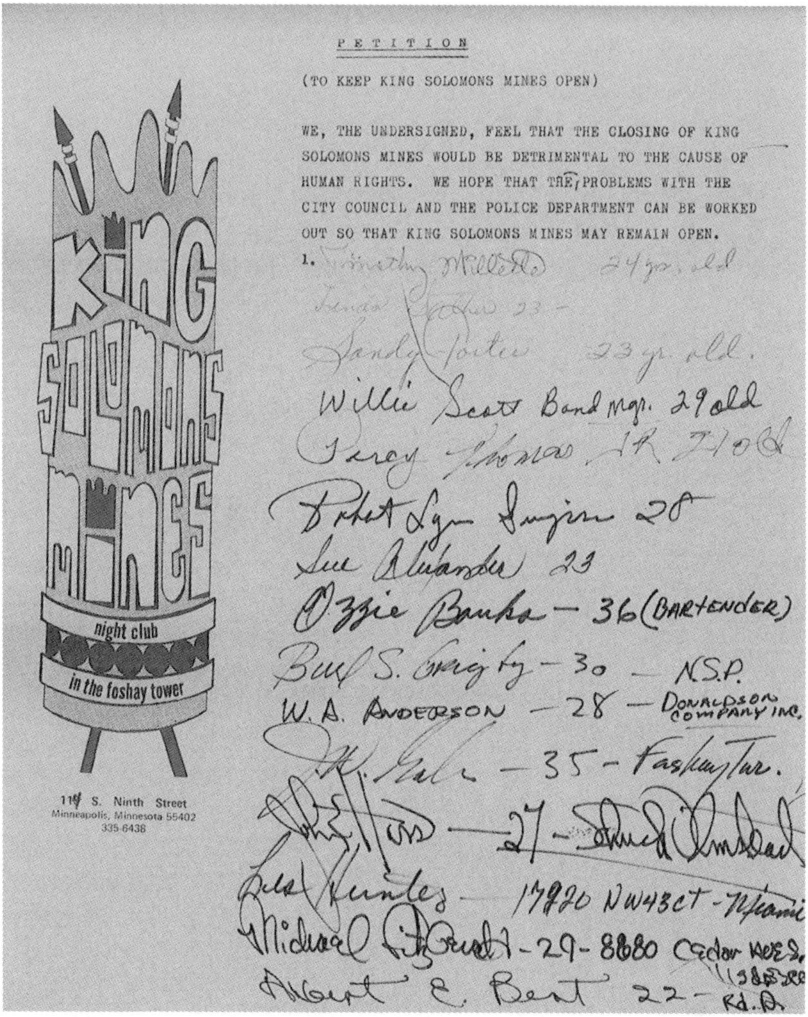

P E T I T I O N

(TO KEEP KING SOLOMONS MINES OPEN)

WE, THE UNDERSIGNED, FEEL THAT THE CLOSING OF KING
SOLOMONS MINES WOULD BE DETRIMENTAL TO THE CAUSE OF
HUMAN RIGHTS. WE HOPE THAT THE PROBLEMS WITH THE
CITY COUNCIL AND THE POLICE DEPARTMENT CAN BE WORKED
OUT SO THAT KING SOLOMONS MINES MAY REMAIN OPEN.

1.

King Solomons Mines
night club
in the foshay tower

11½ S. Ninth Street
Minneapolis, Minnesota 55402
335-6438

A petition in support of King Solomon's Mines included twenty pages of
signatures by regulars of the club like *Star Tribune* columnist Will Jones,
musicians Maurice McKinnies and Willie Walker, and local celebrities such
as Earsell Mackbee of the Minnesota Vikings. The petition was submitted
to the Minneapolis City Council in November 1968. Courtesy of the City of
Minneapolis, Office of the City Clerk.

up fracases seem to cause problems for the licensee as a result of this type of operation."

While the City Council and police employees stuck to using coded language while discussing the connections between "rhythm and blues–type dance" and crime, Constantine saw the scrutiny of his club—the only gathering space in downtown Minneapolis where African Americans felt welcome—as a human rights issue. To further emphasize the importance of having a space for black clubgoers in the city, Constantine tapped Marvin Anderson of the Civil Rights Department to help him make his case in front of the council. After testimonies from Mines regular John Doyle, musician Maurice McKinnies, and University student and King Solomon's Mines waitress Pamela Parker about the importance of the club and their firsthand observation that staff at the venue were diligent about checking IDs, Anderson "told the committee this was one place where patrons, regardless of race or ethnic background, could feel at ease. . . . Mr. Anderson stated that Mr. Constantine was an individual deeply concerned with the community as a whole, and was very sincere in trying to work with the police."

Ultimately, the City Council decided that rather than revoke the liquor license for King Solomon's Mines outright, they would suspend the license for sixty days, giving Constantine time to "either dispose of the business, or find a way to clean up the operation." Jens Christensen was the only City Council member to vote no on the motion for suspension, and he wrote a minority report stating why he felt the license should be revoked. At another City Council meeting two days later, Christensen moved that his Minority Report be substituted for the Majority Report and moved to amend that Constantine "be requested to make the necessary arrangements to dispose of his business during such period of suspension." Both motions failed.

It didn't matter: after one year and eight months of operation, King Solomon's Mines was closed.

Ironically, it wasn't until after King Solomon's Mines closed that the club started receiving some killer press. Aside from the ads that Constantine himself took out in the *Minneapolis Star* and *Tribune* papers, the Mines had only managed to garner a few sentences here or there about its music lineups when it was in business. A year after the club's license was suspended, it became a launchpad for several pieces in the mainstream media about discrimination in the music community. "Black Bands Abound, But Not in Downtown," read a *Minneapolis Tribune* article by chief music critic Allan Holbert on November 9, 1969.

"Most club owners agree that there is a definite, if unwritten segregation policy that keeps black bands out of the Downtown clubs, but they are reluctant to talk about it. They know they could get into serious trouble if their remarks were misunderstood by either the Minneapolis Police Department Morals Squad or by Jens Christensen, the chairman of the City Council License Committee," Holbert wrote.

"Personally I have nothing against the Negro bands," an unnamed club owner tells Holbert in the article. "Their music is great. But they attract so many of the colored that the whites stop coming, and pretty soon you have a colored club, and you name one colored club that's lasted Downtown."

With his liquor license suspended and his hands tied, Constantine spoke freely to the press about what he saw as a great injustice. "I know there were some fights, some quarrels, maybe some robberies around the club when it was open, but this had to be expected, at least at first. It's just like when you're integrating schools. You're bringing some disenfranchised people into a new situation so you're going to have some problems," he told the *Minneapolis Tribune*. "This is where the government can be really hypocritical. In some areas, such as schools, buses, jobs, housing, the government forces you to integrate. I was serving the cause of integration voluntarily, and all the city did to me was harass me and eventually wipe me out. I'll tell you truthfully, until the city develops some sensitivity or understanding toward the problem, no night club owner trying to practice human rights or initiate integration policies can possibly survive."

Even though King Solomon's Mines was closed, the fight wasn't over. In the following years, clubs like Cascade 9 and the Flame went through similar trajectories: black bands would start performing, black music fans would flock to the bar, and within a short period of time the city would intervene and close the place down. The trend was so evident that the *Minneapolis Tribune* published an editorial in its November 12, 1969, issue titled "The 'Great White Way' in Downtown" and asked "Is downtown Minneapolis nightlife for whites only?" But over time, another pattern emerged as well: regardless of how many venues were targeted and closed, the music just kept roaring ahead. As the rhythm and blues movement bubbled up from the underground and started registering on the radar of the larger Twin Cities music scene, the players only got stronger, the bands tighter, and the songs funkier. By the end of the 1960s, behind-the-scenes activists were mobilizing to keep the community pressing forward, and more black artists were cutting records than ever before.

Regardless of everything else that was happening in the world and on the streets, in the words of the Exciters' Herman Jones, "We just kept right on playing."

Chapter Five

BLACK AND PROUD

"**M**AURICE WAS THE MAN."

The year is 2014, and the Minnesota History Center is exhibiting a collection of photographs by the late Charles Chamblis, a prolific photographer from Minneapolis who fastidiously documented the African American cultural community in the 1960s, '70s, and '80s. A well-dressed woman is standing next to me and reaching her hand up to the wall to touch a photograph of Maurice McKinnies, who is decked out in a blue polyester suit, hair slicked into a pompadour, face scrunched in soulful song. Most people touring the exhibit have remained relatively quiet, calmly observing the hidden histories that are unfolding in front of them. But when this woman catches sight of Maurice, her eyes go soft and she sighs and smiles, like she's suddenly being transported back in time.

"He was *it*," she says to me, herself, and anyone else within earshot. "He was the man."

A recording plays overhead of Maurice McKinnies and his band the Champions. The band hammers through a funk groove like a freight train, chugging and grinding relentlessly under The Man's impassioned voice. The recording is lo-fi and scratchy, but if you squint hard enough you can pretend you're back at King Solomon's Mines or the Cozy, shimmying through a packed and sweaty crowd, intoxicated off the stiff drinks and knowledge that this scene exists

on the fringe, that nothing like this has even happened in Minnesota before, that this might be the most swinging scene on earth.

"Maurice was the one," says Wanda Davis, who would occasionally play with Maurice and his midsixties band the Blazers in an all-female backing group called the Blazettes. "He was just so natural with his talent."

Like so many of the groups who were photographed by Charles Chamblis and included in recent compilations of Twin Cities funk and soul music, it makes no sense why Maurice McKinnies isn't celebrated on the same level as influential Minnesota acts like the Trashmen, the Castaways, or even white contemporaries like Willie Murphy. By all accounts McKinnies was the biggest rock star of his time, rivaled locally only by Wee Willie Walker and his Exciters, Napoleon Crayton and the Amazers, and by blazing-hot touring acts like Harvey Scales and the Backsliders.

McKinnies knew it, too. "It's hard for black musicians here," he told *Insider* in 1972. "It's double hard here I should say."

By all reports, McKinnies did everything he could to break through in the Twin Cities. Almost every band he performed with is referred to in hindsight as a *supergroup,* meaning that he hired the most skilled players of his time. He packed the clubs every time he played. He cut two funky, fiery 45s with his band the Champions and sent them to all the local radio stations and media outlets. But all of his efforts were met with a resounding silence from the larger (white) scene. "It's just about impossible to get a record played in this town. KUXL played it some, of course, and both got on some jukeboxes. But I couldn't even get WDGY to listen to it," McKinnies said in 1972, shortly before leaving Minneapolis for good.

McKinnies's talent was evident from an early age. When he was only sixteen years old, he was tapped by the howling blueswoman Big Maybelle, the artist who wrote "Ball and Chain" for Janis Joplin,

Maurice McKinnies performs in a pinstriped leisure suit with epic lapels in 1972. Photograph by Charles Chamblis. Courtesy of the Minnesota Historical Society.

to join her touring band on guitar. He left his home in Pensacola, Florida, to tour around the South and up to Chicago, and by the time the tour wrapped up his family had moved from Florida to Minneapolis, so Maurice followed suit. Maurice was seventeen when he touched down in the Twin Cities, and he immediately dove into the burgeoning black music scene, joining the Big M's with brothers Walker and Buddy Munson, saxophone player Morris Wilson, and a young Willie Murphy. Walker Munson had just graduated from North High School in Minneapolis, and he knew a local engineer who could cut a record for them in his basement and print a thousand copies of it for $500.

Little did the band know that they were about to make history. Their 45, which features the crooner "Silent Lover" and the saxophone-driven instrumental "Get Going," was the first record cut by an R&B group in the state of Minnesota. Last I checked, someone was trying to sell a copy of the record on eBay for $1,000.

Engineer David Hersk vividly remembers working with the Big M's. They were one of only three black groups playing in North Minneapolis at the time (the other two were the Wisdoms and the Velquins), and more than half a century later he's still kicking himself that he didn't hang on to the master copies of their recording sessions. "I wish I would've kept a lot of the stuff McKinnies had written and we recorded—one of his songs that I loved was 'Going Down to the River.' But that's lost and gone," Hersk says. Because they were all so young and inexperienced at the time, the Big M's never made a sound outside of the Near North Minneapolis neighborhood where they lived and played. The old basement studio was in Hersk's parents' house, and when he got married and moved to St. Louis Park in 1963, he left his original acetates behind. Eventually, all those recordings found their way into the trash.

In 1961, McKinnies started a new band, the Blazers. First it was just bassist Steve Crowe and drummer Edgar Murphy joining him, but before they could get much traction going, McKinnies was called to serve in the Army. After a three-year service, he returned to Minneapolis and kept the Blazers going, adding players like Ronnie Scott, Wilbur Cole, and Donald Breedlove. It was this incarnation

Wanda Davis performing at Dirty Girty's in St. Paul in 1969.
Courtesy of Wanda Davis.

of the band that would tear up the dance floor at King Solomon's
Mines and the Cozy, and they became one of the best-known bands
in the black bar circuit. "He was very much in command and in demand," recalls Wee Willie Walker. "We eventually ended up in a rival
competition."

In addition to tearing up the club circuit, McKinnies had also
become a notorious figure on the North Side. André Cymone, who
would form his first band at the age of twelve with a young Prince
Rogers Nelson, recalls McKinnies cruising through the housing projects off Lyndale in a shiny white Thunderbird and rehearsing with
the Blazers in the basement of one of the houses a few lots away

from where he lived. "They used to practice in the projects, and I lived in the projects," André recalls, with a sense of wistfulness in his voice. "I would see his car drive around, and I would run and run and follow, because I knew who he was. Maurice McKinnies! I knew he had a record, and I was so fascinated. I ran, and they went and practiced down in the basement, and I jumped in the window well and watched them practice."

André would have only been eight or nine at the time, but McKinnies's power as a performer clearly made a lasting impression on him; when he recalls the anecdote, he has a tear in his eye. "They had amplifiers—and I didn't even know what an amplifier was," he says. "I didn't know all that stuff then. You'd see that stuff on TV, but I never saw it for real. . . . That was the first time I saw it for real. So I was just blown away. I was just taking it all in. And it was after seeing Maurice McKinnies that I was, like, 'That's what I want to do.'"

McKinnies had the respect of all his musical contemporaries, too. "Maurice was a fun guy and very outgoing—one of the best singers," says organ player Wilbur Cole. "He was a good man, a good musician. And we were working six nights a week." Despite his growing fanbase and rock-solid live band, McKinnies still struggled to emerge from the underground. The civil rights movement was heating up nationally and the fight for black musicians to be able to gig downtown was coming to a head in Minneapolis. He was going to need help.

To make the big time, Minneapolis-grown garage rockers like the Trashmen and the Castaways found a champion in KDWB's Bill Diehl. Similarly, the funk and soul churning out of North Minneapolis and Rondo had their own trumpeter. His name was Jack Harris. Known on his records as Jackie and on air as Daddy Soul, the young radio DJ, recording artist, and record label entrepreneur was a driving force behind much of the recognition that black music received in the late 1960s.

KUXL was a small community radio station based in Golden Valley, just over the border from Near North Minneapolis. Calling their approach DIY doesn't quite capture it: the station was literally run out of an old motel on Plymouth Avenue and scraped by on

Radio DJ, concert promoter, and Black and Proud record label owner
Jackie Harris in the studios of KUXL, 1969. Photograph by the
Minneapolis Star. Courtesy of the Minnesota Historical Society.

donations and advertisements from businesses in the black community. The low-wattage station could only be picked up by radios that
were within a mile of the station. Despite its weak signal and lo-fi
approach, KUXL was *the* place to hear black music on the airwaves
in the Twin Cities. While other stations in town like KQRS played
the big rock and pop hits of the Beatles, Blood Sweat & Tears, Judy
Collins, and Neil Diamond, KUXL spent the afternoons and evenings
spinning a deeply grooving mix of soul music from artists like Sly
and the Family Stone, Aretha Franklin, Smokey Robinson, Tammi
Terrell, Otis Redding, and Minneapolis's own Maurice McKinnies.

In between songs Harris could be heard casting off one-liners,
telling jokes, and talking up local events. "I called myself 'Old Daddy
Soul,'" Harris says. "So I was like a household name, with the shows

KUXL RADIO/1570

HIT LIST

1   BABY BABY DON'T CRY Smokey Robinson & the Miracles
2   GIVE IT UP & TURN IT LOOSE James Brown
3   EVERY DAY PEOPLE-Sly & the Family Stones
4   THERE'S GONNA BE A SHOWDOWN-Archie Bell &
                                    the Drells.
5   CAN I CHANGE MY MIND-Tyrone Davis
6   I FORGOT TO BE YOUR LOVER-William Bell
7   GOOD LOVING AIN'T EASY TO COME BY-Marvin Gaye &
                                    Tammi Terrell
8   I'M GONNA MAKE YOU LOVE ME-Diana Ross,The Supremes
                                    & Temptations
9   RIOT-Hugh Maskala
10 TAKE CARE OF YOUR HOMEWORK-Johnny Taylor
11 BEGINNING OF MY END-Unifics
12 I STOLE SOME LOVE-Don Convay & Goodtimers
13 HEY JUDE-Wilson Pickett
14 MELINDA-Bobby Taylor & Vancouvers
15 SOCK A POO POO-69 Part II Maurice McKinnies
                                    & the Champions
16 SOUL SISTER BROWN SUGAR-Sam & Dave
17 LOOKING BACK-Joe Simon
18 GETTING THE CORNERS-The Toronadoes
19 LIVING IN SHAME-Diana Ross & the Supremes
20 SQUEEZE-Dynamic 7
21 HOMECOOKING-Jr.Walker & the All Stars
22 30-60-90-Willie Mitchell
23 THIS OLD HEART OF MINE-Tammi Terrell
24 THE WEIGHT-Aretha Franklin
25 MY WORLD ENDED THE DAY YOU LEFT ME-David Ruffin
26 GIVE HER A TRANSPLANT-Intruders
27 DON'T DESTROY ME-Margie Hendrix
28 TILL I CAN'T TAKE IT ANYMORE-Ben E.King
29 TWENTY FIVE MILES-Edwin Starr
30 OILY-Jumsy

THE BEST OF SAM & DAVE
Atlantic SD 8218

PICK HIT

COAL MAN-Mick Rice

LAST WEEKS PICK HIT
THERE'LL COME A TIME-Betty Everett

KUXL'S HOT KICKER......
CLOUD NINE-Mongo Santamaria

LAST WEEKS HOT KICKER
SNATCHING IT BACK-Clarence Carter

NEW RECORDS
1   I'VE GOT TO HAVE YOUR LOVE-Eddie Floyd
2   I DON'T KNOW WHY-Stevie Wonder
3   FOOLISH FOOL-Dee Dee Warwick
4   BABY MAKE ME FEEL SO GOOD-Five Stairsteps
5   WHEN HE TOUCHES ME-Peaches & Herb
6   WHO'S MAKING LOVE-Youngholt Unlimited

TOO HOT TO HOLD
I TAKE CARE OF HOMEWORK-Syl Johnson

LAST WEEKS TOO HOT TO HOLD
MY WHOLE WORLD ENDED-David Ruffin

J A C K   H A R R I S

KUXL'S DADDY SOUL

PRESENTS

TOP SOUL THIRTY

A KUXL Radio "Hit List" from February 24, 1969, shows Maurice McKinnies and the Champions' "Sock-a-Poo-Poo '69" at #15 on the local radio charts.

and on the air. It was amazing for the few hours that I was on the air; I came on at one every day."

KUXL started out primarily as a gospel station, and even as it evolved its sound and grew its roster of DJs, the station stuck with a gospel format until after lunch. "They didn't want to lose their religious program 'cause that paid the bills," Harris remembers. But from 1 p.m. until the sun went down, Harris would be on air spinning the latest cuts he received from his friends in the business, like the producers Al Perkins and Syl Johnson, and talking up all the local and touring artists he was booking in town.

Harris was a Chicago native, and by the time he moved up to Minneapolis on Labor Day weekend of 1968, he had already drummed in several bands and recorded a single, "No Kind of Man," with Perkins for Chess Records. He jumped into a job at KUXL feetfirst, and hit the ground sprinting. "I did everything in radio: I typed the logs when the commercial went out, I got to learn all the odds and ends. My interest was not just to be [an] announcer," Harris says. His role quickly morphed into one of a multitalented scene champion, combining his newfound passion for radio with his interest in promotion, songwriting, singing, drumming, and recording music.

"We had a close connection with Jackie," remembers Wilbur Cole, who was playing in Maurice McKinnies's backing band the Champions and would eventually record a 45 with Harris as well. "He did a lot of our advertisement, and he would also go to our different gigs with us and everything, so we had a pretty tight relationship."

Harris was one of many in the community who had observed the discrimination in the club circuit and the marginalization by the local press. One institution that stood out as being particularly exclusionary was the Connie Awards event, which was hosted by Connie Hechter of music mag *Connie's Insider*. Despite the fact that King Solomon's Mines was packed to the gills every night with fans eager to sweat it out to Maurice McKinnies or the Amazers, and despite the fact that Wee Willie Walker had been tapped by Goldwax to record a barn-burner version of the Beatles hit "Ticket to Ride," which would have sent any hip rock fan into a tizzy, the Connie Awards

Soul artist Syl Johnson was a close friend of Jack Harris and helped produce several records for his Black and Proud label. Johnson invited Harris to emcee his concerts in the Twin Cities, and he brought Harris, Gwen Matthews, Maurice McKinnies, and the Blazers to Waterloo, Iowa, for a show at Club Eldorado in 1969. Courtesy of Secret Stash Records.

nominations were almost exclusively reserved for white men and a handful of white women.

In a direct response to the Connie Awards, Harris decided to throw his own ceremony, the Jackie Awards, to highlight the black artists who were being chronically overlooked. Harris made the announcement on KUXL in the late summer of 1969, practically screaming his excitement into the microphone: "For the first time in the Twin Cities, Sunday, August 31, from 6 p.m. till one o'clock in the morning at

Honeywell Hall, 2636 Portland Avenue South in Minneapolis, will be the Jackie Awards. Yes, this three-foot, gold-plated trophy, given to the number-one group in the Twin Cities."

Inspired by the format of the Connie Awards, the Jackie Awards promised prizes for competitors in various categories like best drums, bass, guitar, organ, and horns, the best female and male vocalists, and special honors for the top three rhythm and blues and jazz groups in the Twin Cities. "The first Jackie Awards, given to the black bands in the Twin Cities," Harris exclaimed on the air, working himself into a feverish frenzy and groaning to emphasize the event's importance. "This is going to be something, oooh boy. This is going to be talked about for days and months after. This is gonna be something. A big thing that's going to become an annual affair: the Jackie Awards." The event went off without a hitch, and was by far the most high-profile and organized showcase of R&B bands in the metro area to date.

Even as his career as DJ, songwriter, singer, and promoter blossomed, Harris held down a night shift working for Honeywell, and that gave him the opportunity to rent out the spacious Honeywell Hall in the heart of the Phillips neighborhood of South Minneapolis for his event. Attendees dressed to the nines and danced their way through a whopping seven hours of live music, celebrating the robust local R&B scene and sweating through the Boogaloo. But whereas the Connie Awards received annual write-ups in both *Connie's Insider* magazine and the daily papers, the Jackie Awards barely made a sound outside of KUXL's radius.

The frustration in the community was palpable. It was only a matter of time before musicians would give up and move on to other cities in search of better opportunities and more respect. Just what was it going to take for black artists to break through to the mainstream white music community in Minneapolis? Jackie Harris was about to find out.

In the fall of 1968, James Brown made his first foray into political music with the anthemic call-and-response song "Say It Loud—I'm Black and I'm Proud." By the holiday season, the song had been

Maurice McKinnies *(left)* was photographed many times by
Charles Chamblis, who was clearly a fan of the vocalist and
songwriter. Courtesy of the Minnesota Historical Society.

released both as a single and as part of his Christmas album. By 1969,
it was everywhere: it was the title track of Brown's new album, it
was getting airplay on black radio stations across the country, and it
had become the unofficial anthem of a newly energized Black Power
movement that had blossomed in the wake of the assassination of
Martin Luther King Jr., and the unrest that swept the nation in the
late '60s.

The 45 for "Sock-a-Poo-Poo '69" by Maurice McKinnies and the Champions was one of only five releases issued by Harris's Black and Proud Records. Four of the five singles were recorded and released in 1969. Courtesy of the author.

The lyrics spoke to a lot of the same sociopolitical concerns that Americans are still struggling with today: the economic disparities and cultural appropriation that continue to disadvantage the African American community as well as white society's irrational fear of black men who have the audacity to strive for excellence. While the lyrics generally reflected the struggles of the era, they also seemed to address the specific problems that were plaguing the black music community in the 1960s, namely, the ongoing struggle for any kind of real recognition. With passages like "We won't quit moving until we get what we deserve," it's no wonder it became a rallying cry for a generation of African Americans who had been marginalized at every turn. And as the song made its way onto the KUXL playlist, it's easy to see why Jackie Harris grasped on to three words in particular: *black and proud.*

Harris had met pretty much every gigging R&B musician in town by the time he held the Jackie Awards in August 1969, and it helped him to make the foray into not just spinning songs on air but getting them down on wax in the first place. He had worked up a collection of songs that fit with the times, and he teamed up with Maurice Mc-Kinnies and the backing band the Champions to book studio time and capture these fleeting, funky sounds.

In quick succession, Harris, McKinnies, and the Champions started firing off singles on Harris's new label, Black and Proud Records. The songs go down as some of the grimiest, grooviest, forward-looking R&B music to ever come out of Minnesota. Some of the songs were explicitly about dancing and movement and capture the energy of that era, like the insatiable "Sock-a-Poo-Poo '69." ("It's kind of sexual, as you can imagine," Harris says, laughing. "Working your butt and whatever else.") A track called "Work Your Flapper" was more nuanced. On the surface, it sounded like an ode to grinding it out on the dance floor, but a closer read of the lyrics reveals a deeper perspective. "I know what I was saying now: regardless of how much you made or how hard you worked, they could work you [to] the bone, but you can't take our sound," Harris recalls. "That was what that was about. It wasn't having nothing to do with dancing."

Emboldened by the success of the Jackie Awards and the lightning they were capturing in a bottle in the studio, Harris was ready to make his boldest move yet. If the press wouldn't come to his shows, he'd bring his band and friends directly to the press.

ROBERT PROTZMAN, "BLACK BANDS LET MUSIC TALK FOR THEM IN 6-HOUR CONCERT," *ST. PAUL DISPATCH*, DECEMBER 22, 1969

Lovia Smith, a black singer from St. Paul, feels that maybe color, not lack of talent, is keeping all-black bands from getting better paying jobs in the Twin Cities.

But rather than simply complain, Lovia decided to let his music and the music of other black bands do the talking.

And "talk" the musicians did in a six-hour bash in St. Paul's Holiday Inn Sunday at which there was food, liquid refreshments, plenty of conversation, and a solid four hours of soul, blues, rhythm and blues, jazz, and rock music.

There were more than 30 entertainers providing the music—about 25 musicians, five different vocalists, and two cute, young black dancers doing the new Chicken, the Popcorn, Four Corners and other contemporary pop dances.

"We were going to have a first-anniversary party for our families and friends," Lovia said while waiting to go onstage with his Soul Sensations. "But I thought, and my musicians agreed, that this would be a good chance to state our case to club owners and booking agents, to let them see and hear what black bands have to offer."

So they raised about $400, hired the hall, sent invitations, rehearsed and waited to see who would come.

Reports were that maybe five club operators and the owner of the largest booking agency (they handle about 40 groups) in the Twin Cities were there. Quite a few musicians, white and black, also were in the audience.

Connie Hechter, publisher of the largest music-only magazine in the Twin Cities, *Connie's Insider,* thought the idea a promotional gem. "It's a great way to make a point," he said. "There ought to be more of this kind of thing in the Twin Cities."

Other groups performing in the for-free concert were The Exciters and Maurice Mckinney and the Champions.

Whether or not there's a human relations problem in music here, and whether or not, if there is, some progress toward solving it was made as a result of the concert, could not be determined immediately.

But one thing was agreed upon by just about everyone there and summed up by one satisfied listener. "There's a helluva lot of talent here and they put on a great show."

The write-up from Bob Protzman was a major breakthrough for black artists in the Twin Cities scene and for the metro media in general. Protzman recalls that this was one of the first times that black artists had ever been acknowledged by either of St. Paul's papers (the morning edition of the *Pioneer Press* or the afternoon *Dispatch*), and that it was a struggle to even get a story like it past his editors. "I got there in 1967, and I had to ask to cover black people, to cover Negroes, as we called them then, because the newspaper wasn't covering them," Protzman recalls.

His article about the concert and the realities facing black musicians was a watershed moment: not only was it a much-deserved spotlight on a bustling underground scene thirsty for attention, but it was also the first time that local music being created by black artists was being discussed based on its merit and content, and not the fact that it had provided the background sound track for a fracas or police sting at one of the town's ill-fated live clubs.

Even still, it heralded a strange new era of arts journalism in Minneapolis, one in which white male journalists at outlets ranging from the daily papers to underground music magazines spent a great deal of time wringing their hands about the "Black music problem," as many headlines hailed it, throughout much of the early 1970s. Well-intentioned as their efforts may have been, the tone of their coverage provides a peculiar, smudged lens through which to look back on the era; rather than talk specifically about Jackie Harris or Maurice McKinnies or any of the dozens of other tremendous soul, R&B, and funk groups that continued to flourish in the beginning of the next decade, the media seemed more focused on the musicians' oppression than on their actual work.

It became such a worrisome pattern that the cause was taken up by Human Rights Commissioner Conrad Balfour, who served from 1970 to 1971 before moving to the Urban Coalition of Minneapolis as executive director. Balfour took to *Insider* magazine in June 1971 to pen an editorial titled "Conrad Balfour on the Black Musician Problem":

> We can all scream about how deplorable this condition is. What I can't understand is how these cats keep their patience. If I were a horn-man, I'd be picketing, stomping, laying down in front of doors, playing my toot in the streets and corporate lobbies and charging admission to white song men playing my music.

Outwardly, musicians plying their trade does not seem to be too difficult a problem. It doesn't take long to find how complex, muddy and frustrating this whole situation is. The booking agent knows enough not to pass a black rock group off to a club. They'd turn him down. The club owner knows if he employs a black group he will draw mixed audiences. The police will insinuate that the club owner is jeopardizing community safety, and crack down harder on underage customers than at other clubs. The club owner becomes afraid of losing his license . . . Meanwhile Milwaukee, Indianapolis, Chicago and New York wonder what the fuss is here. They dig good music and hire blacks without fanfare.

If you're a law enforcement agency like the Department of Human Rights, who do you prosecute? The mayor? The city council? The club owner? The booking agent? Some say one, some the other. I believe all are responsible.

Or to put it more succinctly, in the words of writer Dave Hill, who interviewed Maurice McKinnies shortly before he left Minneapolis for the San Francisco Bay Area: "You can walk from Plymouth Avenue to Hennepin in twenty minutes, but Maurice hasn't been able to make that move in ten years."

Chapter Six

•

THE FLAME

BACK IN THE 1950S AND '60S, when you were walking north on Nicollet Avenue toward downtown on a clear evening, you could see the giant neon cowboy coming from a few blocks away. With his wide-brimmed hat aglow and his arm stretched out in a wave, the cowboy would greet you as you approached the Flame Bar and Cafe, beckoning you into the city's biggest and brashest country bar. Opened by the Jewish brothers Abe and Ray Percansky (aka Perkins) following the repeal of Prohibition in the 1930s, the Flame was Minneapolis's answer to the Grand Ole Opry: in its main room, a five-hundred-seat dinner theater boasted a hydraulic, self-rising stage; in the back room, a bar had space for another few hundred guests and another smaller band.

By the late 1960s, the Flame had become one of the most highly respected country music venues in not just the Twin Cities but the entire nation. The club's bookings would be regularly cited and discussed in the latest issues of *Billboard*, and regular guests on stage included Patsy Cline, Loretta Lynn, Carl Perkins, Buck Owens, and the Carter Family. Back in those days, you could also catch sight of four or five cowgirls from Ardis Wells's Rhythm Ranch Gals dancing and kicking their way through a set on top of the bar, and another Minnesota-reared country star, Sherwin Linton, became a house band with his rockabilly act the Fenderbenders.

In the 1970s, the Flame on Nicollet Avenue and Sixteenth Street gradually transitioned from a country bar to "disco soul," showcasing R&B bands like the Philadelphia Story, Haze, and Prophets of Peace. The club operated from 1938 until 1978. Photograph by Jack Gillis. Copyright 1978 Star Tribune.

When the Flame flipped from an all-country format in August 1972 to a more wide-ranging booking policy, the venue split down the middle and embraced a surreal new dichotomy: each night there would be a country band on one side of the building and an R&B band on the other, and more open-minded patrons could wander from room to room to sample two very different ends of the musical spectrum. For a period in the mid-1970s, the Flame was *the* place to see the latest funk and soul music in the Twin Cities, thanks in big part to a house R&B band that held down Friday and Saturday nights for two years straight. For a music community that had been shuffled from bar to shuttered bar and subject to seemingly endless downtown nightlife politics, the Flame became the latest safe haven for an entire scene of black music fans.

When Wee Willie Walker participated in the first incarnation of the Valdons back in the early 1960s, he had no idea that his band's name would reemerge and persist through another decade-plus of soulful expression. Although Walker and his bandmates parted ways when the decade was still young, the Valdons moniker would come back around the dawn of the '70s and be embraced by a whole new generation of soul singers. Although their roots were firmly planted in the Midwest, the second incarnation of the Valdons met in an unlikely place: Pensacola, Florida, where singers Clifton Curtis, Maurice Young, and Monroe Wright all were stationed in the Air Force.

Clifton was a South High School grad who had lived in Minneapolis since the age of eight, and he grew up watching the original Valdons—with Willie Walker, Timothy Eason, Joe Dibiaso, and Jimmy Crittenden—rehearse in their practice space when he was a preteen. He was too young to join the group then, but by the time he enlisted in the Air Force in 1966, he knew he was meant to start a vocal group of his own. With memories of those early Valdons performances still lingering in his mind, and the suspicion that no one in the Pensacola area would have ever heard of the Minnesota group, Curtis decided to name his new group after the band that inspired him. The band moved to Mobile, Alabama, and started working the club circuit. After about a year of touring around the South and calling themselves the Total Sound, a new generation of the Valdons was born.

As soon as they got out of the military, Curtis talked his fellow Air Force servicemen into moving north to Minneapolis, the land of freezing cold winters and a smoking-hot underground music scene. But the band was already used to a certain level of success down in Mobile, and trying to integrate into the local scene proved frustrating. Like so many black groups of their era, the first time the Valdons received media recognition for their group, it was in an article about how much trouble they were having finding steady work. In a cover story for *Insider* magazine's Black Artists issue, members expressed frustration over their lack of higher profile gigs in white clubs. "Until you're known, you're nothing, and if you're black, you're less than that. You know, we're really being blocked out," member Bill Clark told the magazine.

After touring around the South with the Valdons and other groups, Clark said that Minneapolis clubs were far more racially segregated than anything he'd encountered in other cities. While other major cities like Atlanta or Dallas would book the band to play in white-owned and white-frequented clubs, allowing them to pull in massive crowds, he noticed that the Twin Cities seemed to keep its black talent sequestered in off-the-beaten-path spaces that drew smaller, entirely black audiences. "You ask about getting a job, and the first thing they say is, 'Well, try the Cozy, or check over at Dirty Girty's,'" he said. "That's fine if you want to remain on a rock bottom level, that's it. If you want to do something nationally and be recognized, well, that ain't hip. We've worked hard at it, to become national, and we don't want to settle for the bottom of the barrel."

The Valdons had just added the superstar vocalist Napoleon Crayton of the Amazers to their lineup, they had a blazing horn section, and they had a manager. They'd just recorded a 45 at the new Sound 80 studio in South Minneapolis, with an original from Crayton, "All Day Long," on the A-side and a song by renowned guitarist Donald Breedlove, "Love Me, Leave Me," on the B-side, and their live show was stronger than ever. Still, they felt stuck in limbo between the underground scene and a national market that was hungry for bands just like them.

Napoleon Crayton, an elder statesman of the group, had a broader perspective on the difficulties black artists were perennially battling in Minnesota:

Everybody says you've got to leave Minnesota to make it, but I see it the other way: I see that you can make it in Minnesota, but

The Valdons recorded their first and only 45 at Sound 80 in 1971 and released it on the short-lived Twin City Movement label. Two years after releasing the single "All Day Long," written by lead singer Napoleon Crayton, Crayton would leave the group, and the band would evolve into the Philadelphia Story. Courtesy of Secret Stash Records.

they're going to keep the doors closed for some more years and run off all the youth. That's why Minnesota doesn't get recognition as having entertainers now. Let's say your group, or some other group, Pride and Joy, anybody, makes it. It's going to be hard for them to stay in Minnesota because Minnesota isn't really getting behind them and pushing them. So I think that the problem of it is that until somebody with some kind of power opens the town up a little bit, we're going to be in trouble. We're going to be forced to move on soon, if we can't get work.

Regardless of their frustrations, all five members of the Valdons who were interviewed agreed that their love of the music kept them pushing forward. "I think the reason I stay in music is because I just like to do it," Curtis said. "It makes me feel good when I can get up in front of an audience and sing something, and see the people feeling what I'm singing and enjoying it. I like to think I'm pretty good at it. Every time I get up on stage I try to give the people the best of me that I can, because each time that I do, I've conquered something inside myself."

Tired of being shuffled around or sidelined, the Valdons were in need of a place exactly like the Flame. It had not just local but national prominence and respect, it could draw both white and black audiences, and its owners were just starting to expand into booking new styles of music. The neighborhood where the Flame sat—which is now referred to as Stevens Square Park—was changing dramatically in the early 1970s, thanks to the recent construction of I-94, which sliced a wide path through the Flame's backyard. Many of the more upscale restaurants in the area migrated up Nicollet Avenue to get closer to the heart of downtown, while the cheap rent around the nearby Loring Park neighborhood brought together a cross section of artists, hippies, and lost souls looking for cheap thrills. Times were changing rapidly, and the Flame knew it would have to adjust its business to keep up with the desires of the neighborhood.

"The Flame was huge for us," recalls Gwen Matthews, who cut her teeth singing with Maurice McKinnies and the Blazers before being recruited by the charting country-rock group Crow, which morphed into the band Colla. Because she was performing in a more rock-leaning band with both white and black members, Matthews had started playing a wider variety of venues and performing for mixed audiences; many of the R&B artists who would play the Flame after her in the mid-'70s credit her for opening the door for more black musicians to perform. She explains:

I got involved because I was in a really, really good band. It was the Colla band, working there. And I think when I met people that I liked or recommended, that would leave the door open for them to get a spot. I had some ins and outs that some people didn't have. I wasn't singing in the so-called black neighborhoods; I was everywhere. I started in them, as I worked at the Cozy Bar on the North Side, and as I worked with Maurice McKinnies, but as I started changing, the bands I was performing with were blended—they were mixed bands. And not even thinking about it, it was sometimes easier to be in a cultural blended band than it would be to be in an all-black band. All-white bands didn't have any worries. But black bands, you know, they were always concerned about . . . who the customer would be. So if you were in a blended band, you kind of attracted everybody.

And I wasn't a person who thought about racial anything. I did not think of myself as anything but a female singer who loved to do what she did. So I didn't think of myself as a black female singer, or white female singer. Just a singer.

Looking back on his memories of playing with the ever-evolving Valdons, Maurice Young—who was a founding member of the group in their military days and rejoined the Valdons in 1973, replacing Napoleon Crayton—credits both Gwen Matthews and the Percansky brothers who ran the Flame for giving his band a shot. And it turned out that the Valdons and the Flame were a match made in polyester-suited heaven. "We packed five hundred people into that club every single weekend—every night of every weekend for almost two years straight," Maurice recalls, sitting next to his wife, Nona Young, for an interview in 2015. Both Maurice and Nona were instrumental to the Flame back in those days. Nona was a DJ and helped the band manage its show calendar, while Maurice sang in the group and did the band's bookkeeping.

Not long after the Valdons started holding it down every weekend at the Flame, a scene started to develop. As with King Solomon's Mines, the Flame brought together all kinds of R&B fans from all kinds of backgrounds, from college students and hippies to hustlers to middle-class businessmen and players for the Minnesota Vikings. "Carl Eller, Alan Page used to come to watch us. Smokin' Joe Frasier used to come and see us. He was one of our biggest fans," Maurice recalls. "Our audience, when we played at the Flame, was a mix of people. It was fifty-fifty [white and black]. It really was, and it was great."

Maurice McKinnies sings as fans dance to the sounds of his Blazers at the Cozy Bar on Plymouth Avenue, 1968. Photograph by Mike Zerby, *Minneapolis Tribune*. Courtesy of the Minnesota Historical Society.

The Valdons' Napoleon Crayton, Monroe Wright, Bill Clark, and Clifton Curtis *(left to right)* pose with a stuffed tiger for a publicity photo to promote their 1971 single "All Day Long." Courtesy of Ricky Washington.

As the crowds grew, the band got more and more serious about their stage show and their wardrobe. Most nights they would be ready with one or two changes of clothing, swapping out white tuxedos for black ones or picking out different-colored shirts for each player. Maurice says that their matching outfits were heavily inspired by the Temptations, with an added early-seventies flair of glittery, disco-inspired bling. "Some [clothing] we were able to buy over the counter, and others we had made," he recalls.

"You can't buy that many sequins and studs in the store," Nona laughs.

"Those had to be put on by hand—glued on, in some cases, or sewn on," Maurice adds.

The fact that they were so detailed about their uniforms isn't all that surprising, considering that the Valdons were a group of guys who met in the Armed Forces. Going onstage was their version of reporting for duty.

"They always kept that military mentality—they always have," Nona says.

"We were always on time, and we always carried ourselves as gentlemen," Maurice adds. He looks at his wife and smiles sheepishly. "Even when the women were crawling all over us, we still tried to be gentlemen."

Another one of the Valdons' founding vocalists, Monroe Wright, recalls just how unique it was that an all-black R&B group was able to play to mixed audiences at a more upscale club:

> Somehow or another we managed to make the Flame our home. Because of the type of clubs we played when we first came out of the blocks, I believe that we got pigeonholed. We opened at the Cozy and Peacock Alley. Those were dives. . . . The upscale clubs had a hard time booking us because our crowd was going to follow us wherever we went, so they were tentative, to say the least. But we got into the concert promotion business. We managed to meet people that were business people. And we knew how to promote ourselves and promote what we were doing using the media.

Musically, too, the Valdons wanted to break out of the black music world and appeal to a wider array of music fans. "We had a crossover mentality," he says. "Our objective was to be a crossover group, not just a straight R&B group. We liked music by the Spinners. We would do arrangements of songs like 'The Way We Were' or Carole King's song 'Let Me Be the One.' We were a real vocal group, in the tradition of the Temptations and the Four Tops. And we had showmanship."

After just a few months of playing steady gigs at the Flame, the Valdons had traveled a long way from the despondent outlook of their early 1972 interview with *Insider*. They had developed a sizable fan base, they were earning steady income, and they were heading to New York City to cut a new 45 for H&L Records—home of Van McCoy and the Stylistics. Although their first 45, "All Day Long," had landed on the Hot 100 charts when it debuted in 1971, the Valdons were having trouble gaining traction in the larger industry. H&L promised to offer the band the big break they deserved and made arrangements to have the Valdons record at the historic Sigma Sound studio in

Philadelphia. That 45, which featured the songs "People Users" and "Gotta Get Back," captures the aesthetic of the Valdons during their Flame heyday. And it seems to vent some of their feelings about the false promises and sideways deals they'd so far encountered in the major label industry.

Over a hiccuping near-disco beat and driving wah-wah guitar, Clifton Curtis opens the song with a spoken-word preamble and warning: "The people we're talking about are those that use others just to get a little higher in this world. Not meaning any harm, of course, but someone always gets hurt. . . . So if you fall into this bag, you'd better start checking yourself out." The band's distinctive four-part vocal harmonies are present in the song, but you can sense the band being pulled in a more modern direction, embracing the slapping bass lines and strut of funk music, and the synthesized strings of disco.

Because they had made the recordings out East, the band decided it was time for a name change to go along with their new label and new recordings. They switched from the Valdons to a name inspired by their auspicious time spent in the City of Brotherly Love. "Our manager said, 'Your story began here in Philly. You ought to change the name; maybe the Philadelphia Story,'" Wright recalls.

Maurice Young has a less pleasant memory of his time in Philadelphia that is woven into the time when they changed their name:

> On our way to the studio I'm driving my 1972 Pontiac, and we get pulled over by the police. There's our manager, Stan Weiss, and his partner Jeff Reuben sitting there next to me in the front seat, and the other three guys were in the back seat. They wanted to know if Stan and Jeff were all right—if we had kidnapped them. And they made everyone get out of the car and get on the ground.
>
> When the police officer first stopped me, I had my foot on the brake, and he says, "I need to see your license and registration." I said, "It's in my glove box here." Stan was sitting on [the gearshift]. So my car inched forward just a bit, and next thing I know he had a gun at my head. "Freeze!" I threw my hands up and I started shaking. I said, "I'm not going anywhere." I put it in park.

"I'm not going anywhere." And then we told him we're a singing group. We're on our way to Sigma Sound to record. And that was what happened when we went to record our first song.

When they got back to Minnesota, they told the story to everyone they knew. Their brush with racial paranoia became their story about Philadelphia, and their new record was poised to bring them from the Twin Cities to the world. When the 45s were issued by H&L Records and the song "People Users" debuted at #76 on the Hot 100 charts, the song was credited to the Philadelphia Story.

Ironically, given that their new single directly addressed the band's caution of "People Users," the band's new label wanted to seize the moment and enter them into a controlling contract in order to promote their 45. "They called us to New York, and they presented us with about an inch-thick contract, which we brought home to Minneapolis with us and had it checked out," remembers Wright. "They wanted everything that we would ever own in our dreams and power of attorney just in case they needed some money if we were out of town, whatever. So we said we couldn't sign the contract, so they gave us an ultimatum. Either sign it or the deal is trash. We blinked and they pulled the record off the market."

With dreams dashed once again, the Philadelphia Story returned to Minneapolis and put their full efforts back into promoting concerts at the Flame. At this point, members say they were holding down six nights a week at the club, trading stage time with the horn band Sweet Taste of Sin. "Only night off was Monday," Wright recalls, shaking his head. "It was such an exciting show that it was packed almost every night."

As the de facto house band, the members of the Philadelphia Story got an intimate look at just how unusual the Flame was. "The Flame was a strange place. It was two different worlds in one building," Wright says. "On one side there was country-western, and on our side, we were the R&B. So if you stumbled and went to your left and ended up on the country- western side, you realized you were in the wrong place. We charged a nice cover charge, which was about

The Philadelphia Story, featuring *(left to right)* Bill Clark, Monroe Wright, Maurice Young, and Clifton Curtis, perform with the backing band the Sweet Taste of Sin. The two bands would often perform together billed as Sweet Story. Photograph by Charles Chamblis. Courtesy of the Minnesota Historical Society.

$5, which was a heavy cover charge in the '70s. It was a fashion show every night. People would come dressed, and everybody with new cars and everything."

Each night would open with the eight-piece Sweet Taste of Sin band, which Wright describes as "just like KC and the Sunshine Band—twirling horns and dancing. Plus most of them sang lead, so when they would open the show, it would just be incredible." Once the stage was properly warmed up, the Philadelphia Story would come out for a set, doing call-and-response chants with the audience like James Brown and getting the whole room moving across the dance floor. Clifton Curtis would choreograph complex dance moves to keep the crowd engaged, and Monroe Wright would often do the splits. On the more swinging nights, Pharoah Black of KMOJ would come down to introduce the band, yelling into the mic, "Ladies and gentlemen, the Twin Cities' own power and the glory, the Philadelphia Story!"

"The stage came up out of the floor: it would rise up," Wright says. "They had the main stage, and then the part where we came out front was oval shaped, and it was hydraulically lifted up four feet off the floor, and you could dance on both sides. Before show time people danced in front of the stage, but when we came up, it came up out of the stage and then we'd come out, and it was game on."

The Philadelphia Story would give the stage back to the Sweet Taste of Sin for another forty-five minutes and come back out to play for forty-five minutes more. And they'd repeat the formula night after night after night. "Every night it was intense, and we got better and better. We wore uniforms. Everybody came there. And then after that, we'd go party."

During their residency, the band also got to know the two characters who were running the joint and who had an unusual past of their own. "Abe and Ray Percansky—they were the owners—and they took me into their office once. There was a picture on the wall of both of them standing with one foot up on this 1938 . . . It was one of the old gangster cars, and they each had a machine gun," recalls Maurice Young. "They used to be the bodyguards for Kid Cann. I'll never forget them. They were something else."

"Abe and Ray were from back in the gangster days," Wright agrees. "I wanted to buy my ex-wife a nice ring for her birthday, with a diamond in it. And the next thing I know I'm sitting in his office—Ray's office—and he opens this safe and pulls out a little box and lays out a black velvet cloth and dumps a pile of diamonds out about this high," he says, holding his hand several inches off the table. "And then he starts giving me lessons on how to pick out the best stone, and carbon and highlights and all of that, and he sold me three-quarters of a karat for $150. I bought him out and I was all good. Kisses and everything."

"I remember Abe walking through there—little short guy and gruff little guy," adds Young. "He'd like to kick people in the butt when he'd kick them out the door: 'Get the heck outta here!'"

chs
dances
to
the
purple
haze

CENTR

The revered funk band Purple Haze (who would record as Haze) are captured by a yearbook photographer from Minneapolis Central High School while performing at a school dance in 1973. Photograph from the 1973 *Centralian* yearbook. Courtesy of the Hennepin County Library Yearbook Collection.

The Philadelphia Story wasn't the only band to make the Flame their home in the mid-1970s. Other progressive funk bands could be spotted in the club's Zodiac Room, like Prophets of Peace and Haze, which each passed through the Flame on their way to recording notable albums at ASI Studio and playing larger festivals and headlining gigs in town.

The way Sonny Knight remembers it, there wasn't one particular style of R&B happening at the Flame during that time, as the genre was splitting wide open and incorporating elements of psychedelic and prog rock into its woozy, bluesy sound. Knight moved back to the Twin Cities in 1974 after a stint in San Francisco and jumped headfirst into playing with Haze, which had quite the buzz going

An advertisement for Purple Haze placed by its management company, Schon Productions, Inc., in *Insider* magazine, 1972.

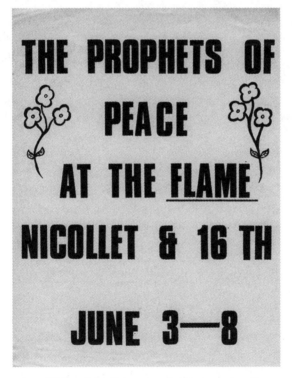

A beautifully minimalist poster advertises a series of shows by Prophets of Peace at the Flame, mid-1970s. Courtesy of Secret Stash Records.

For the band's 1976 press kit, Prophets of Peace posed for photographs at the Como Park Conservatory in St. Paul. *Left to right:* Moribik Abdul (percussion, vocals), Bruce Palaggi (saxaphone), Earl "Sonny" Williams (keyboards, vocals), John Curlee (trumpet), Dave Dahlgren (guitar), Anthony Scott (bass), Roland Atkinson (trombone), Stephen "Brother" Bradley (drums), John Gregersen (saxaphone). Courtesy of Anthony Scott.

around their ASI-recorded debut and their breakout single, "I Do Love My Lady."

"Haze would come out with stuff that we made up in our heads and had a seamstress put together, with polyester and gigantic bell-bottoms and flashlights—like you would see Sly Stone or Earth, Wind & Fire come out with onstage," Knight recalls. "Whereas [the Philadelphia Story] would come out looking like the Temptations or the Stylistics, or somebody of that era."

Prophets of Peace was also embracing a more crossover sound, as evidenced on the 1975 single "The Max," which mixes complex jazz-oriented rhythms into a grooving funk vibe. With the support of KUXL airplay, the band would quickly go from playing runs of shows at the Flame to performing in front of twenty-five thousand rock fans at KQRS's Concert for Sharing in the summer of 1976.

In its final years, the Flame was frequented by the North Side teenage band The Family, which would be one of the last acts to play the main stage. "We ended up kind of closing that place up," recalls drummer Joe Lewis. "We were in our prime—seventeen, eighteen [years old]. [It turned out we] were playing the last two weeks of that place closing up. It needed to close. They had a dressing room in the basement, and we didn't even change there. We were too scared. It was just like a basement nightmare."

"I didn't like it, I remember that," says Sonny Thompson, the bass player in the Family. "The pimps were in the front, and as you come in and go to the back of it, that's where the regular people would go. It was really crazy, because it was like big pimpin' in the front. They were still playing country in the front, but the pimps would still be there. Like, what's going on? I'd never been in a place like that." Lewis agrees: "In the early '70s it got to be like pimp avenue just right there off of Nicollet."

During this time the neighborhood around the Flame had continued to shift and become something of a no-man's-land, a barren stretch of random restaurants and parking lots that felt disconnected from both downtown and the south-bordering Whittier neighborhood that would soon spawn some of Minneapolis's most influential punk bands. By 1981, crime in the area had seeped into the Flame as well, and the city pulled the venue's liquor license and shut it down. "I've been in business here forty-one years, and I think the punishment was far too severe for the crime," owner Abe Percansky told the *Minneapolis Star* in 1981. He continued:

I think I should have been warned or told to change my ways. I've never been in trouble or arrested before. Here I am, seventy-five years old, and I've held public licenses all my life. I'm getting blamed for all the uncontrollable types around here. The prostitutes on the avenue, it's littered with them. We haven't had a walkin' policeman on this beat for four or five years. That's a police problem, isn't it? What do they expect when they take fifty thousand housing units out of here, put a freeway through, and make a ghetto of the neighborhood? And I get blamed for it.

Steve McClellan, who would manage First Avenue from the late '70s through the mid-2000s, remembers speaking with Percansky about the Flame after it closed. As Percansky told him, "The city gave me this neighborhood, and I just wanted to give the neighborhood someplace where they felt welcome."

Chapter Seven

•

BLACK AND WHITE

LTHOUGH MINNESOTA HAS STRUGGLED for decades with segregation and inequity—in 2015, Minnesota was ranked dead last in a study of wage and achievement disparities nationwide—there is also a long history of musicians from different parts of the Twin Cities finding common ground through music. The first band from Minneapolis that combined black, white, and Latino members dates back to before the civil rights movement swept the nation or the unrest of the late 1960s hit North Minneapolis. In fact, it dates back to the birth of rock 'n' roll itself.

Following in the footsteps of the many Mexican American immigrants who came to Minnesota in the 1930s and '40s, Augie Garcia came up in St. Paul's West Side Flats, a low-income residential area that sat just across the Mississippi River from downtown St. Paul. The West Side Flats were a multicultural melting pot, similar to housing in North Minneapolis in the midcentury; the neighborhood was originally settled by Jewish American immigrants, and over the years it became home to a growing number of Native American, African American, Lebanese, and Syrian citizens as well. So it didn't seem all that unusual for Garcia to pull together a band of neighborhood kids from the West Side who happened to come from different backgrounds. The Augie Garcia Quintet ended up being historic for several reasons: they recorded what is widely regarded as Minnesota's

Augie Garcia performs with bassist Maurice Turner at the West Seventh
Street Rec in St. Paul. Courtesy of the Minnesota Historical Society.

first rock 'n' roll record in 1955, "Hi Yo Silver"; they were so ferocious live that they actually got yanked off stage by Elvis Presley's manager while opening for the King; and they were the first of many bands from Minnesota that would combine disparate ethnic backgrounds and influences to unlock new sounds.

Like all good stories about Minnesota music, the players from the Augie Garcia Quintet can be connected to many other notable artists from the past sixty years. Augie's piano player, James "Cornbread" Harris Jr., still performs around town to this day and is the father of the famous Minneapolis Sound alumnus and producer Jimmy Jam (aka James Harris III). Augie's bassist, Maurice Turner, was the uncle of a talented young kid from Near North named Prince Rogers Nelson. We can all marvel at the fact that decades before Prince and Jimmy Jam would attend classes together at Bryant Junior High in South Minneapolis, their relatives had already commingled on stage and laid down a barn-burning single that received radio airplay. It's not the only time that the kids who would put Minneapolis on the map in the 1980s would appear destined to work together: Prince's dad, pianist John Nelson, would play in a jazz trio with André (Cymone) Anderson's dad, the bassist Fred Anderson, years before the two youngsters would meet and form their first band together, Grand Central.

Cornbread Harris cowrote "Hi Yo Silver" with Garcia, and the song is an excellent example of the way they merged their two backgrounds. "Cornbread really brought the rhythm and R&B to the band and Augie brought the Mexican to it," said Joe Minjares, who wrote a play about Garcia's life for St. Paul's History Theatre in 2015, in an interview with *MinnPost* columnist Jim Walsh. Reflecting on his career in 1989, Garcia also stressed how significant Harris's contributions were to his sound: "He used to make the band really cook. A lot of these things you hear on the records were his ideas, which were excellent ideas. . . . He had that kind of natural built-in rhythm that I really liked." The Augie Garcia Quintet was the first in a long line of bands that not only embraced the idea of integrating different cultures and styles but thrived because of it. The quintet helped usher in a new era of music in Minnesota—one spearheaded by a new

Although their sons wouldn't know it until years later, Prince's dad, John Nelson (seated at piano), and André Cymone's dad, Fred Anderson (upright bass), performed together in the Prince Rogers Trio, making the young musicians' meeting seem predestined. Photograph by John F. Glanton. Courtesy of the Hennepin County Library.

generation of young artists with electric guitars, basses, and drum kits, and one that found an immediate audience with the booming population of teenagers who were eager to dance to live rock music.

With the exception of the Andrews Sisters and polka artists like "Whoopee" John Wilfahrt, the early 1960s marked the first real period of commercial success for musicians in Minnesota. As Elvis's swiveling hips were still haunting parents' dreams and the Beatles' mop tops were making their way across the pond, a slew of young bands like the Trashmen (with their song "Surfin' Bird") and the Castaways (with "Liar, Liar") started climbing the charts and handily filling up ballrooms around the region. The Trashmen were an especially interesting case study in what made music successful in the early 1960s. Their big hit "Surfin' Bird" was a note-for-note mash-up of two previously released songs by a black doo-wop group from the West Coast called the Rivingtons, "Papa Oom Mow Mow" and "The Bird Is the Word." The Rivingtons struggled to chart either of their songs when they were released in 1962, but the Trashmen found immediate success with their remake, showing just how eager the Twin Cities pop radio market was for R&B-meets-rock sounds from clean-cut young white artists who could connect with the metro area's large population of suburban teenagers. And connect they did. The influx of attention and cash caused the local rock scene to explode, and for the first time the artists making contemporary music in Minneapolis could be heard on the radio (KDWB) and could be followed in daily newspapers and specialty magazines like *In-Beat* and *Twin City 'a Go Go*.

But not everyone was invited to the party. In a pattern that still persists to the present day, the music community in the Twin Cities seemed to be split along racial and ethnic lines. In 1965, the city's most powerful booking agent, Dick Shapiro, estimated that there were 350 bands in the metro area "good enough to get away with a dance job." Shapiro and similar booking agents were sending these young rock bands all over the state, from school dances to small-town armories and ballrooms to large rooms like St. Paul's Prom Ballroom. Even after the Trashmen and Castaways proved that teenage local rock bands could draw fans to ballrooms by the hundreds, soul music was less of a guarantee for bookers. Despite the national success of soul groups like the Impressions, Temptations, and Martha and the Vandellas, it was uncommon to hear black R&B and soul artists coming across Twin Cities airwaves. During the week of March 6, 1965, for example, the Temptations' song "My Girl" had skyrocketed to the #1 position on the *Billboard* Hot 100 charts and could be heard on most Top 40 radio stations in the country—except for the Twin Cities' KDWB, whose top songs that week were by Gary Lewis and the Playboys, the Righteous Brothers, Roger Miller, and Petula Clark.

The scarcity of soul and R&B music on the radio made it nearly impossible to promote that kind of music live. And so groups like

Dave Brady and the Stars, pictured in an *In-Beat* magazine article in March 1967. As one of the Twin Cities' first interracial R&B bands, it comprised three African American vocalists, Dave Brady, Wally Lockhart, and Jimmy Lawrence *(front row)*; and a mostly white backing band that included bassist Bill Brisley, trumpet player Mark Skok, saxophonist Carl Bradley, drummer Tom Hoth, and guitarist Bill Lubov *(back row)*. Courtesy of Steve Kaplan.

the Exciters, the Amazers, and the Bluejays were mostly booked to play shows in their own neighborhoods of Near North and Rondo, while bands like the Underbeats and the Avantis were sent out of town in a touring van to play towns across greater Minnesota. All of which made it even more remarkable when a group named Dave Brady and the Stars, which featured four black vocalists and a mostly white backing band, started making waves in the larger Twin Cities concert market in 1965.

Not unlike many of the early R&B groups from Minnesota, Dave Brady met fellow vocalist Wally Lockhart when they were walking home from classes at Central High School in South Minneapolis. After a bit of impromptu singing in the streets, Brady invited Lockhart to his basement for a rehearsal with a few of their Central High classmates; half of the group happened to be white, and the other happened to be black. The trio of singers—Brady, Lockhart, and Jimmy Lawrence—harmonized vocal melodies in the style of their favorite groups like Sam and Dave, and the Impressions, while the backing band channeled everything from the garage rock and rockabilly of the larger Twin Cities scene to the jumping basslines of R&B.

The group decided to try playing in public for the first time at Magoo's, a pizza parlor on Nicollet Avenue and Lake Street in South Minneapolis, and the teenagers had low expectations. "Less than ten people were in attendance to begin with, and after three or four songs the place was empty," guitarist Bill Lubov told Secret Stash Records in 2011. "The audience must have run out and told their friends, because a half hour later the place was packed!"

Encouraged by their auspicious debut, the band got to work refining their sound and their performance. As was common in that era, Dave Brady and the Stars put just as much (if not more) time into their clothing, dance moves, and onstage flair as they did their arrangements and songs. "The importance they attach to clothes can be seen in the fact that they believe that they can't afford a truck for their equipment (they pile it into their cars) but they recently spent nine hundred dollars on clothing for a single show," the journalist Steve Kaplan wrote in his *In-Beat* magazine profile of the group. Vocalist Lockhart justified the expense: "To other bands this may sound stupid, but that one day, and two or three weeks after that, we made a very big impression. We thought clothes would be of a more immediate concern to our audience than a truck. Clothes more directly affect what we are to our audience."

By signing with a major booking agency, Dave Brady and the Stars fell into a larger touring circuit—which set the band apart from others coming out of the North Side that could barely get a gig outside of their own neighborhoods. Soon, they were working the same small-town schools and dancehalls that were being frequented by the Underbeats and the Castaways. "Of course, when we started we wondered if we would make it in this kind of circuit," Dave Brady told *In-Beat* in 1966. "But, with one exception, we haven't met any real discrimination. I think we were more self-conscious about it than anyone else." Vocalist James Lawrence added: "If we go into a small town, and they have never seen a Negro, the initial reception is sometimes cold. They really don't know what to expect, because they have been told so many lies. It is left to us to leave an impression, and destroy any stereotypes about Negroes they might hold."

The group eventually made its way into the studio, recording three songs just down the street from Magoo's in the basement space Nic 'O' Lake Records. The 45 for "Baby, Baby I Need You" serves as a good time capsule of the band's skills: the three vocalists seamlessly blend their falsetto harmonies into a perfect doo-wop style. If the date on the album didn't read 1967, you could easily mistake it for a recording from a decade prior. On the flip side, a cover of Curtis Mayfield's "Ridin' High" churns with an angular urgency, the bopping bass and aggressive drums hinting at the grimy funk music that would soon sweep the underground scene. The success of Dave Brady and the Stars in the latter half of the 1960s told a new story to the musicians in the Twin Cities: R&B music wasn't just for black artists anymore, and the more they melted down the boundaries between race and genre, the more exciting the music could become.

Sometimes, when pondering the Minneapolis Sound, it starts to feel like an intricate braid that keeps getting thicker and more colorful as more threads are woven in. In the 1950s, there were only a few threads: gospel, doo-wop, jazz, R&B. Each sound was carefully crossed over and under the others, neatly dovetailing together. In the 1960s there were threads of garage rock, folk music, psychedelia, funk, and the blues, each adding a new strand of color to create a vibrant swirl. And by the 1970s those threads got all kinked and knotted up and downright weird, pulling in everything from the Afrofuturism of George Clinton's Parliament to disco to the earliest traces of spoken word that would presage hip-hop.

One shining example of an artist who helped weave woozily psychedelic new threads into the sound is Willie Murphy, who came up on the North Side of Minneapolis playing guitar in R&B groups like the Big M's, the Nobles, and the Valdons. "I was the proverbial only white guy in many of those bands," he recalls. He split for the University of Minnesota campus after high school and helped launch the West Bank folk and blues scene that bloomed in the late '60s. The first music Murphy released under his own name was a collaboration with folk artist "Spider" John Koerner, who was one-third of the influential group Koerner, Ray and Glover, and who made a big impact on a young Robert Zimmerman when he was attending the U of M in 1962 and frequenting folk music showcases at the 10 O'Clock Scholar.

Koerner and Murphy put out a phenomenal album together called *Running, Jumping, Standing Still* in 1969 on Elektra Records, which had already released several successful Koerner, Ray and Glover albums. Though they set out ostensibly to create a folk album, Koerner found a creative foil in Murphy, whose deep knowledge of music theory and passion for experimentation had them pushing and pulling their melodies and chord changes in all kinds of unexpected directions. The album saw great success and had Koerner and Murphy touring all around the country, including a spot opening for Jefferson Airplane. At one point Murphy was even offered a major-label deal with Warner Bros., the same label that would sign a young North Minneapolis kid named Prince Rogers Nelson just a few short years later. But Murphy turned it down and oriented his sights back toward the local scene in Minneapolis. "I toured with Koerner through the '60s, which was a high time, that was kind of the folk circuit," remembers Murphy. "But my roots were in rhythm and blues. So I came back here to start a big R&B band."

Murphy's vision for his band was simple: he wanted as many people onstage as possible, encouraging as much dancing as possible. Beyond that, it was anyone's guess where the wind might blow his new group. "I wanted to have a big R&B band that did the kind of music I like, which is original music, dancey, political, everything. And that's what we do: it's R&B, very jazzy, with horn parts. It's a big rhythm-and-blues band, to dance to and to listen to. And everybody sings," Murphy says.

When Willie and the Bumblebees formed in 1971, it was a heady time for the Twin Cities music scene. The Depot, which would later become First Avenue, had just opened in downtown Minneapolis, and more bands of Murphy's era were graduating from the teen ballrooms and dance halls to playing the bar circuit. Hippie culture had permeated the nightlife scene, especially on the West Bank, and Willie and the Bees were testing boundaries in several directions: they were an interracial band at a time when that was still quite uncommon; they flaunted the fact that they were hard-boozing partiers; and they were insistent on playing entire sets of their own music instead of cover songs. "There was a big impetus, coming out of the '60s, that you could play original music, in bars and so forth. We were one of the first ones to do it. And we played in clubs where people didn't do that," Murphy recalls. "Downtown was pretty straight-laced back then; there were bands that played downtown six nights a week and did all cover material. But the West Bank was loose. We could play there."

The West Bank of Minneapolis—named after the West Bank of the University of Minnesota campus and the fact that it was situated on the western shore of the Mississippi River—had a built-in audience of college-aged bar-goers looking for an excuse to cut loose and soak up the cultural scene. The Bees gravitated toward a biker bar there called the Joint, a bigger venue next door called the Cabooze, and the Firehouse, which would later be occupied by the Mixed Blood Theater. "All these [gigs] were wild dances where people took

Willie and the Bumblebees, as depicted on the back of their debut album *Honey from the Bee*. The band's raconteur sax player and vocalist Maurice Jacox missed the photo shoot, so the band literally copied and pasted him into the bus window later—a testament to their loose, funky ethos. Photograph by Mark Peterson. Courtesy of Secret Stash Records.

their clothes off and everything," Murphy says, letting out a bashful chuckle. "Back then, people did that. And I remember it fondly, although I got a lot of backlash from certain people who didn't like that. It wasn't my fault, you know?"

For a better understanding of the wild antics of those early days, one needn't look further than the headline of a cover story about the band in *Insider* magazine in December 1971: "Boozing with the Bumblebees." The article begins as reporter Tom Murtha meets up with the band at the 400 Bar on the corner of Cedar and Riverside in the heart of the West Bank neighborhood and follows them as they shoot pool, drink straight whiskey out of a bottle tucked into the belt of saxophone player Maurice Jacox, and wander over to their practice space down the street. Looking back on it decades later, it provides an excellent time capsule of the band's spirit, camaraderie, and idealistic view of the world. When asked about the group's over-all direction, trumpet player Voyle Harris responds, "Cosmic vibrations." Jacox simply replies, "Badass."

"Yeah, that was Willie and the Bees. That was exactly Willie and the Bees," Jacox says in 2014, shaking his head and laughing as he reflects back on that "Boozing" article and his time with the band. "It was absurd. We were lucky to have lived through it." Jacox met Murphy when they were attending high school together at Minneapolis Central, and they met back up on the West Bank when Jacox returned to Minneapolis from spending a few years in San Francisco. Murphy was recruiting performers from throughout the rock, jazz, and soul scenes, including the vocalist Willie Walker (who only played in the band for the first few months of its existence, handing off lead vocal duties to Murphy), keyboardist John Beach, saxophonist Gene Hoffman, drummer Stephen Bradley and guitarist Russell Hagen (both of whom, like Murphy, had played in an incarnation of Dave Brady and the Stars), plus Jacox and Voyle. In addition to being a constantly growing and fluctuating band, they also roamed the West Bank like a gang, refining their reputation as notorious rabble-rousers.

"We were part of a West Bank crowd of musicians and pseudo-intellectuals and drunks and pool shooters who hung around the Triangle Bar and other places," Jacox recalls. "We were arguably, back before it was in fashion, the drunkest and most outrageous band to ever come out of the Twin Cities or Minnesota. Going to a Bee gig was an event. People wanted to see who'd still be standing at the end of the night—usually, it was most of us and not them." He continues:

There are literally books that could be written about the Bee years. There are anecdotes that would just have you laughing till tears ran down your face. In the fifteen-year run of the band, we did things that very few bands have done musically. Everyone in that band, for all that drunkenness and stupidity—even though most of them were alcoholics and ended up going into treatment for addiction of one form or another—everyone in that band was extremely intelligent. Extremely. That's part of what was so great: that we weren't a bunch of drunken dummies.

We were a bunch of brilliant people who chose to get drunk and express ourselves through our stupidity. Jesus, does that sound good in print?

For all the antics onstage, the real chemistry of Willie and the Bumblebees came alive in the recording studio. Their first experiences recording together happened in an unlikely place: at a summer camp on an island in the middle of Lake Minnetonka, where Willie Murphy was producing the debut album of an up-and-coming young songwriter and slide guitarist named Bonnie Raitt. It was 1971, Raitt had just inked a deal with Warner Bros., and she was looking for a producer to help her record her debut album. She had gotten to know Murphy while he was passing through Boston on tour with Koerner. Before she knew it, she was roaming the West Bank bar scene with Murphy's crowd in Minneapolis. "Bonnie came out here and stayed at my house. We actually slept together in the same bed and went out every morning looking for a good place to put the studio to make the record," Murphy recalls.

"After about four or five days of cutting a swath through the West Bank, drinking and shooting pool, talking shit and talking music, Bonnie pretty much decided, 'Yeah, these are the guys I want to do my album with,'" Jacox adds.

"We were lucky: we found this big summer camp at Lake Minnetonka, which was vacant, and it was perfect. It was a holiday, you know," Murphy says. He estimates that Bonnie and his Bumblebees stayed on the island for about a month, recording to four-track tape with the help of Koerner, Ray and Glover bandmate Dave Ray. Murphy adds: "People would get up in the morning and fish off the dock. After a couple of weeks of more or less horsing around—but I was actually kind of getting the music together—Bonnie said, 'Don't you think we should start recording?' And we did. And I think it's a really good album."

Bonnie Raitt is a laid-back, almost lackadaisical blues record, and you can practically see Willie and his Bees sprawled out in the studio, arranging horn parts on the fly to accentuate the soulful sound of Bonnie's slide guitar and her sweet, youthful voice. A cover of

Bonnie Raitt *(far left, on chair)* with Willie Murphy *(stairs, top right)* and his sprawling Bumblebees crew, eating grilled corn on the cob between recording sessions at Camp St. Vincent on Lake Minnetonka, where the group recorded her debut album, *Bonnie Raitt.* Photograph from *Insider* magazine, September 1971.

Murphy and Koerner's "I Ain't Blue" anchors her connection to the pair of Minnesota icons, and John Beach's nimble piano playing and the orchestrated punch of the Bees' horn section on "Finest Loving Man" capture the charisma of a young band that was just figuring out how to harness its sound.

The same year that *Bonnie Raitt* was released, a prominent recording studio was in the process of moving into its new facilities in South Minneapolis off Twenty-sixth Street and Minnehaha Avenue, just a half-mile south of the Bees' West Bank stomping grounds. Known as Sound 80, the studio promised to usher in a new and more professional era of recording in Minneapolis. "The first building in Mid America designed and constructed specifically for work in the art of recorded sound is now in full scale operation," an article in the April 3 edition of *Connie's Insider* proclaimed. "Included in the building's 12,000 square feet of floor space are three recording studios, a special studio for recording and mixing sound for motion pictures, an electronic music studio, a mastering laboratory for production of masters or 'molds' for pressing records and a production shop for the development, design and manufacture of specialized sound systems."

The Twin Cities had no shortage of recording studios already, like Cookhouse, on the corner of Nicollet and Twenty-sixth Street in South Minneapolis, which began as Kay Bank Studio in 1957 and was the site of historic recordings like the Castaway's "Liar, Liar." But Sound 80 took the whole game up a notch. Helmed by the German-born composer, jazz musician, and audiophile Herb Pilhofer, who had worked at Kay Bank, the studio aimed to host not just local rock bands but also choirs, orchestras, commercial composers, and avant-garde electronic artists. Pilhofer poured $200,000 into outfitting the space with the most cutting-edge equipment available. "Half Buck Rogers spaceship, half Robert Indiana painting come to life, it's a technological dream, a rocker's paradise, a fantasy world of flashing lights, twisting knobs, surrealistic sounds and spinning discs," *Star Tribune* reporter Mike Steele raved just before Sound 80 opened.

By the time Willie and the Bumblebees headed to Sound 80 to record their second album, *Out of the Woods,* they had solidified their position as a West Bank institution and the studio had been elevated to a revered stature in the music community. Bob Dylan had used Sound 80 to record new versions of five songs that would appear on his acclaimed 1975 album *Blood on the Tracks.* Cat Stevens chose the space to record his 1977 album *Izitso.* And Twin Cities funk bands like the Band of Thieves, led by veteran players Napoleon Crayton and Donald Breedlove, were using the space to record their albums. Bill Gaskill, who played tenor saxophone with the Band of Thieves, remembers his visit to the studio vividly:

> There was an ad on the radio that said, at Sound 80, $1,000 for ten hours of recording. That was a big deal. So we played a gig

to pay for that. We go there and we record an album in a day—
ten hours—all the tracks, all the vocals, and a mix, because that's
how well-rehearsed we were. We rehearsed nine hours a day, six
days a week. We walked in there and nailed it all in one take. Bob
Dylan was there when we were doing it.

Because Sound 80 had several large studio spaces, it wasn't uncommon for musicians to cross paths in the hallways between recording sessions. But Gaskill's memories of wandering through the
space at the same time as Dylan just might take the cake. "We were
in Studio A because we needed the big room. Bob Dylan was in Studio C," he says, recalling that Dylan had returned to Sound 80 for
a session in 1976 following the runaway success of his *Blood on the
Tracks* recordings, especially the single "Tangled Up in Blue." (Dylan
was likely there recording his parts for a contribution to the song
"Sign Language" for Eric Clapton's album *No Reason to Cry*.) Gaskill
goes on:

> He came out for air, and by this time the horns were laying our
> parts. He was a big star, about as big as you could get. And here he
> is, in our control room. David Rivkin, David Z is the engineer. And
> we're knocking these things out. The horns are double-tracking
> everything, so next, next, next. We've got like an hour left. So
> we're just plowing through the stuff. And Dylan's watching.
> . . . . So I'm playing, and everything that you'd think would be
> going through my mind is going through my mind. And then
> in between songs the door opens—there he is. He doesn't say
> anything. He just walks to the front of the window, up against
> the wall. The tape starts again: "Okay, let's start playing." And he
> stays for the entire session. And at the time I'm thinking, "Does
> he need a horn section? Are we going to join his band?" And we
> get done, and I'm thinking, "What's he going to say?" But he's just
> a dude. He's just a guy, right? So he goes, "Any of you got weed?"

In 1978, Sound 80 made its biggest splash yet: it became the first
studio in the world to record to digital tape, thanks to its proximity

to the tape's manufacturer, 3M. The St. Paul–based tech company had just built the 3M Digital Audio Mastering System, and before they made it available for distribution they gave a prototype version to engineer Tom Jung at Sound 80 to beta-test its capabilities. The first recordings captured on digital tape were of the jazz group Flim and the BBs, and the St. Paul Chamber Orchestra, which would win three Grammys for their recording of Copland's *Appalachian Spring*. And the first modern rock or R&B group to get into the studio to try out the digital system was Willie and the Bees. "Nobody had ever made a digital record yet of pop music or R&B or anything like that, so we were first," recalls Murphy. "When we finished the album, there was a big reception, and they had a lot of industry people, because of the idea of digital."

Bob Dylan, the Band of Thieves, and the Bees wouldn't be the only Minnesotans to utilize Sound 80 during its heyday. A young Prince Rogers Nelson would also spend significant time in the space learning his way around recording equipment in preparation for his debut album, *For You*. But we're not there quite yet. Before Prince could head into the studio, he would need to be introduced to a generation of musicians who would open the door for him to forever memorialize that Minneapolis Sound.

Chapter Eight

THE FAMILY

We were all close, like brothers.

—JEFF TRESVANT, aka JT Apollo

IT SPEAKS VOLUMES that the first event ever to be held at The Way in North Minneapolis, which occurred the next day after the first civil unrest in the summer of 1966, happened to be a dance party for neighborhood youth who needed a safe space to gather and get down. By the early 1970s, The Way's role as a community center, educational facility, and safe haven had been solidified. But its lasting legacy in the Minneapolis community just might be its music program, which was founded almost immediately after opening the building to young people in the area. "The Way is in the initial stages of developing an Arts Program," a proposal from early 1968 reads. With major funding secured from Twin Cities business owners like Raymond Plank, The Way had the opportunity to invest significant money in its cultural programs and began by launching a summer arts program in 1968.

Thousands of dollars were poured into purchasing not just instruments like a piano, drums, and guitars, but also a portable stage, amplifiers and speakers, a lighting rig, and a counter for serving soft drinks and coffee. In other words, The Way was being outfitted as

Families from the Near North neighborhood gather for a street party outside The New Way. Photograph by Charles Chamblis. Courtesy of the Minnesota Historical Society.

a space where music wasn't just practiced but also performed—and soon enough, young musicians from the area would be vying for their time onstage. A line from the budget proposal for that first summer arts program seems to foreshadow the potential of providing such serious resources to young artists: "The Way Arts Program has been designed . . . *to reach those individuals for whom lifetime careers in the arts are a possibility* and provide an opportunity for them to discover their potential for original creative work."

Boy, did it ever. Looking back on the legacy of The Way now, that's one area where the center not just met but exceeded its ambitious goals. As the musicians who hung out at The Way tell it, the opportunities the center offered them in their youth opened a door in their minds to the possibility that they could devote the rest of their lives to music.

The Way was so integral to the drummer Joe Lewis's upbringing that he has a hard time remembering life without it. "I actually started working at The Way when I was about thirteen years old, and it was right after the riots," he recalls. "They had some community program about cleaning up the neighborhood. So when I was about thirteen, I worked there during the summer, and I grew up in that environment." Lewis was enrolled in The Way's Project Big Sweep, which employed teenagers in the area to head out into the surrounding neighborhood to clean up the streets. With funding from the Office of Economic Opportunity, The Way hired roughly 170 youth between the ages of fourteen and eighteen to perform services "like mowing lawns, cleaning alleys, removing garbage, and clearing play areas for Northside residents," A. Karim Ahmed wrote in *Inside The Way*. "All day long one could see the broom brigade leave and return with their shovels, wheelbarrows, brooms, and rakes. In between work projects, classes in basic skills and minority history were required of all the participants."

Project Big Sweep epitomized everything The Way stood for in its formative years. It was taking a radical, hands-on approach to engaging black teenagers with their neighborhood, and mixing community service with classes about African cultural history and recreational outlets ranging from sports to theater and music. The center's programming served as both an incentive and a respite, offering supervision and a safe gathering space, but also the freedom for teens to dictate their own activities and interests.

For Joe Lewis and his friend Sonny Thompson, that interest was always music. Thompson recalls starting to play a variety of instruments from the early age of eight or nine. "I was a piano player first, and then I was a drummer, and then I ended up playing the guitar, because my dad ended up buying me a Fender Stratocaster," he says. "I was playing mostly R&B and jazz, I was listening to Jimmy Smith and Wes Montgomery and all that, and my mom loved classical music. But then one day this Jimi Hendrix album accidentally came from the Columbia Record collection, *Axis Bold as Love*. And that was it. I was like, 'Man, I'd never heard no sound like that on the guitar. I gotta learn how to do that.'"

He and Lewis would get together and listen to the latest albums from Jimi Hendrix and James Brown, developing their ear and fiddling around with any instrument they could get their hands on. When The Way opened, it was a revelation for two aspiring young musicians: the community center had a music room with all kinds of different equipment, and it was all just waiting to be explored and played. When they talk about their memories of The Way now, everyone from Thompson and Lewis's generation speaks of that music room in the same way. They all call it "that back room," recalling how it was tucked away in the far corner of the building, past all the meeting rooms and makeshift offices. That back room was where the magic happened.

Lewis says it didn't take long for the back room to become their new favorite place to hang out. Before long, they were heading to The Way every day, putting in long hours of rehearsal time. "Me and Sonny Thompson, we grew up real close to The Way. We lived on Logan Street, probably about two blocks away," Lewis recalls. "All of our parents knew we were being pointed in the right direction. Because that community center, it kept us out of trouble, and trouble was all around us. But when you've got a purpose—you've got nice instruments—you go in the back room, work on music four hours out of the day, it was something really to look forward to every day."

One by one, Thompson and Lewis added more musicians to their evolving jam sessions and started forming an official band, calling themselves Back to Black. The Way's resident music director, Harry "Spike" Moss, became the band's de facto manager and would mentor the group as they solidified their lineup and worked up a set list of the latest R&B, funk, and rock songs. By the early 1970s, Back to Black would be The Way's reigning house band. "Spike Moss was instrumental," recalls Lewis. "He was a director, but he was also our manager, so he ended up pretty much putting the group together from there as I got to be a young teenager."

* * *

Remarkably, even though he was only fourteen when he started rehearsing at The Way, the organ player Pierre Lewis was already heavily involved in the local jazz scene by the time he joined the Back to Black band. "Pierre was a child prodigy," Joe Lewis says. "We found Pierre when he was young. We were probably, like, fifteen and sixteen, and Pierre really wasn't a freshman in high school yet."

"I was probably doing gigs ever since the seventh or eighth grade," Pierre recalls. "The guys I was playing with at that time were in their thirties, and I was playing the organ at the time, a Hammond B3, and it weighed 435 pounds. So those guys would have to move my organ for me." When Pierre came to The Way, he was already connected to a lineage of influential jazz players who would come to teach music classes at the center. He explains:

> Jerry Hubbard, he's my cousin, and he was one of the best guitar players in the Twin Cities. And I was already affiliated with Bobby Lyle, even before I came to The Way. . . . I was about eleven years old, and I was playing at this place called the Legion in St. Paul, and my mom had to come with me because I was so young, and Bobby Lyle was in the audience. And he was like, "Yeah, it looks like I've got some competition." Which he really didn't, you know, but he was just trying to inspire me.

In addition to gigging around St. Paul, Pierre would also visit the Blue Note in North Minneapolis, where his uncle was the bar's owner. He met the organ player Billy Holloman at the Blue Note when he was thirteen and continued being mentored by Holloman throughout his career. "He took me under his wing. From the day he met me, he was like a big brother, mentor, everything," he says. All of which meant that by the time Pierre made his way to that back room at The Way, he was helping the other young musicians to make connections to the previous generation of jazz and soul musicians.

Bobby Lyle in particular had climbed to the status of nationally revered musicianship in the early 1970s, having left St. Paul to spend most of his time on the road in support of his jazz-pop group Young-Holt Unlimited (a collaboration with Redd Holt and Eldee Young of the Ramsey Lewis Trio). By 1974, he had broken out as a solo artist and toured all over America and Japan, was racking up major awards from musical competitions, including the Yamaha International Organ Contest, and had been enlisted as the newest member of the genre-melting funk-rock group Sly and the Family Stone. When he would return to Minneapolis, Lyle would head to The Way, where he would hold jam sessions and workshops with the jazz guitarist Jerry Hubbard and his drummer brother, Gene. As his own career blossomed, it was obvious that Lyle remained passionate about shaping the minds of the next generation and ensuring that a wide array of musical genres remained in the pop music lexicon.

"A thing was born a few years ago called black radio, which usually can be found on the extreme right hand of the dial, and whoever programmed that music felt blacks could respond to only one kind of music—the funkety-funk, get on up stuff—with some DJ shouting in between the records," Lyle told *Insider* magazine in 1972, unquestionably speaking about Minneapolis's right-hand-of-the-dial AM station KUXL. "They'd better get themselves together, because as a result of what they're doing young blacks are exposed only to this, and when you ask if they dig Charlie Parker, they say 'Who?' They've never been exposed to jazz. And that's a tragedy."

Lyle's teaching made a lifelong impact on the young musicians frequenting The Way. In fact, many members of the house band cite it as one of the ways they gained an edge over the other fiercely competitive bands in their community. "Jazz is something you study, and most R&B players can't play jazz," says Pierre Lewis in an interview. "Jazz, you have to study that for a lifetime. It takes a lot to be a good jazz musician. So I had a little bit of an advantage over most of the guys who played keyboard, because they were just playing R&B. I was playing R&B, jazz, and blues."

For the young players at The Way, cross-pollinating different genres wasn't just a creative choice: it was a tactic they knew would help them stand out from a sea of new bands that were emerging from their immediate surroundings. "Man, there was so many bands," Sonny Thompson recalls. "You know, everybody was trying to put on a show. We came out, and we was rock, funk, Parliament Funkadelic, Sly and the Family Stone, Jimi Hendrix, the whole nine. We tried to do as much stuff as we could. Jackson Five, and all of it. We tried to do as much music as we could and just crowd it in."

By the time Back to Black solidified their lineup they had grown to include seven members, including a horn section that pulled in players from South Minneapolis in addition to the North Side. The way that trumpet player Jeff Tresvant (known by his stage name JT Apollo) tells it, the band had started rolling through Minneapolis like a snowball and picking up every talented player it could. He recalls:

> I was playing with a band called Brainstorm at the time, another young band from over South Minneapolis. But who discovered me was Sonny Thompson. Sonny Thompson saw me coming out of my house, and I happened to be going to a rehearsal with Brainstorm. Some guy jumps out from a tree and scares the holy heck out of me. I'm like, "Are you crazy? What are you doing?" He says, "I'm just playing with you. I see you're carrying a horn case. You're a horn player?" I said, "Yeah, I'm a horn player." He said, "I'm with a band over in North Minneapolis, and we are looking for horn players. Do you think you might be interested?" I said, "Of course, I'm interested." So I skipped going to practice [with Brainstorm] and went to practice there. We took the bus crosstown all the way from South Minneapolis to North Minneapolis, and that's exactly how I started.
>
> I had no idea it was at The Way or where it was at. I really too much didn't care. And then once I got there and saw how into the music those guys were, how professional they were, and I'm like, "This is it; this is where I want to be."

Tresvant invited his friend Ronald Bronson to come sit in on saxophone, and soon enough the two players were busing up to North Minneapolis every day after school to rehearse with Back to Black

Not long after the band formed— and when members of the group were only fourteen to seventeen years old—Back to Black was invited to perform at the Walker Art Center auditorium for a concert on January 5, 1972. Courtesy of the Walker Art Center Archives.

at The Way. "There was a North Side thing and a South Side thing. I don't think I would've went over there by myself trying to get in the band," recalls Bronson, noting that he was only fourteen when he joined Back to Black and that the unrest that swept North Minneapolis a few years earlier was still fresh in everyone's minds. But once he got to The Way, he realized that everyone who rehearsed there treated the opportunity like a privilege. "You couldn't come in there doing wrong things. Spike was really the one that made sure of that," he says. "It was really more professional to me than I had ever seen. You had to be at practice on time, and sometimes you'd get roughed up if you weren't doing the right things, or if you were late. You'd get a little chastising. But they liked me and they wanted me to be on the right track. They knew that I was a juvenile, and Spike knew that I was in his hands."

Around the time that Tresvant and Bronson came on the scene,

Organ player Pierre Lewis, drummer Joe Lewis, and bassist Sonny Thompson
rehearse in the famous back room of The New Way in the mid-1970s.
Courtesy of The Family.

Back to Black would also decide to change its name. "Having the name Back to Black, that kind of knocked us out of a lot of opportunities, because people would think we were militant or something," Pierre Lewis recalls. "If part of your name has *black* in it, there's a lot of places you weren't going to be able to play. So we switched the name to The Family."

Their new name spoke to the camaraderie of the evolving group, which also included Randy Barber on guitar, Calvin Cyprian on keyboards, Bill Perry on saxophone, and Roland Willis Jr. on vocals. The older members kept an eye on the younger kids, and the group bonded over marathon rehearsals together in the back room. "At that time, we would rehearse all night. All day, all night," Thompson says. "Because we were just kids, I mean, I love my mom, but she knew I was doing music, so she knew where I was at. She knew I was there. So she was cool."

It didn't take long for The Family's reputation as an intensely well-rehearsed, genre-blurring show band to spread to other aspiring musicians in the neighborhood. "It's real funny because Terry Lewis, Jimmy Jam, Prince—everybody came through there," says Tresvant. "We were kind of the base band there, or the house band there, and I learned so much stuff from those guys."

"We were trendsetters," remarks Joe Lewis. "Guys like André Cymone, Jimmy Jam, Terry Lewis, they used to come to that back room. It was an open-door policy. I can remember Terry Lewis coming and he wanted to learn some songs. He came and sat in [for] probably two or three days of rehearsing and then got some songs down, and he ended up taking them off and being another band that spun off. André Cymone, same thing. He'd come down, watch us, slap on the bass, play with me for a while, move on."

On Friday and Saturday nights, The Family would transition from rehearsing to performing, holding dances in the cavernous back room of The Way for a few hundred teenagers or more. And one of The Family's first higher-profile gigs was at a big Battle of the Bands summer showcase outside the Phyllis Wheatley Community Center, not far from The Way.

The Family performs outside The New Way during a summer festival.
Courtesy of The Family.

"There was a time when blacks weren't invited to come to the Aquatennial Parade—they were pretty much getting beat up when they would attend—and so we started having a festival at the Phyllis Wheatley, and it just drew droves of people," remembers Joe Lewis. After the incident at the Aquatennial Parade in 1967 between black women and white attendees that erupted into a night of unrest during that particularly volatile summer, many members of the black community had stopped attending it all together. The Phyllis Wheatley provided North Side residents the perfect alternative to the downtown parade: it was situated in the heart of the Near North neighborhood, and it already had a decades-long history of providing a safe space to African Americans in Minneapolis as both a settlement house and community center. "They had a big field in the back, and it was where a large number of people could gather and didn't need a big city permit on the community center's land. That was a big nice event. Even Prince ended up playing at that event," Lewis recalls. "It was one of those places where as young entertainers

The Family, featuring Pierre Lewis on keyboards, Joe Lewis on drums, Jeff Tresvant on trumpet, Bill Perry on saxophone, Sonny Thompson on bass, and Randy Barber on guitar (pictured mixing on sound board), perform a sound check at the Metro Lounge in St. Paul in 1977. Photograph by Charles Chamblis. Courtesy of the Minnesota Historical Society.

we came together for the people and gave them something. It's like medicine to relax you."

If those Battle of the Bands showcases at Phyllis Wheatley had been staged anytime after 1985, tickets could have easily been sold for a couple of hundred dollars a pop. But back in the mid-1970s, before the sounds of North Minneapolis had been declared to be the new Minneapolis Sound, it was a free showcase of all the up-and-coming teenage bands in the area: The Family; the hard-driving Afrofuturistic funk band Flyte Tyme, which was led by the respected saxophonist David "Batman" Eiland and anchored by bassist Terry Lewis; Jimmy Jam's Philadelphia soul–inspired vocal group Mind & Matter; and a new band featuring Prince Nelson and André Cymone called Grand Central.

16 Insight Wednesday, August 9, 1978

Communicative Arts

Northside Festival draws 6,000

A newspaper clipping from the August 9, 1978, issue of *Insight* depicts the massive crowds at the sixth annual Northside Summer Fun Festival outside the Phyllis Wheatley Community Center. The 1978 lineup included Sounds of Blackness, Flyte Tyme, Mind & Matter, Quiet Storm, and Prince, who would return home a few short months later to make his official solo debut at the Capri Theater. Courtesy of Secret Stash Records.

The incentive for besting one another at these Battle of the Bands showcases wasn't something as superficial as money or trophies: they were competing for neighborhood notoriety. "It wasn't for money. It was just who got the most claps—you could tell. You knew who was the best, when you got the applause, and people would tell you," says Bronson.

"No, there was no prize," says Pierre Lewis. "Everybody wanted to outdo, to sound better than the rest of the groups. It was real competitive." When asked where that competitive spirit came from, Pierre doesn't hesitate. "Everybody wants to be the best," he insists. "Everybody wants to be Number 1. And you've gotta look at it this way, too: I was automatically competitive from playing sports, and Joe played sports, and if you look at Flyte Tyme, Terry Lewis, he played for North High, he played sports. So we all were competitive. We all wanted to be the best. It was just something that was in our blood."

The Family would eventually make their way into the studio, recording at the legendary Sound 80 in South Minneapolis and hiring

Prince to fill in as a session player on backing vocals and guitar. In fact, it was the money that Prince made playing on The Family's song "Got to Be Something Here" that would buy him a plane ticket to New York City in 1976 to start sniffing around the major record labels. And it was Sonny Thompson's guitar and Pierre Lewis's organ that could be heard all over the demos that Prince made for his debut album, *For You*, which he borrowed from The Family members after leaving his equipment with his Grand Central bandmates.

Although he rarely spoke of it publicly, The Family's influence on Prince reverberated throughout his career. When Prince would form a new side project for Warner Bros. in 1985 following the success of *Purple Rain*, he would name the band The Family. And Sonny Thompson—whom Prince lovingly called Sonny T. and looked up to like an older brother—would tour the world with his New Power Generation and remain friends with Prince until his untimely passing in 2016.

When I ask Sonny if he thinks it's a fair assessment that he mentored the generation of musicians who get credited for the Minneapolis Sound, he smiles bashfully and nods his head:

Yeah, I think so. Prince and André used to hang outside my basement window while I'm down there rehearsing. I'd be, like, "Well, why don't you guys just come on in and jam?" Me and Prince used to jam a lot because I had all my equipment, because the band [The Family] had broken up at that point. I had all this equipment in my basement, so I would just sit on this mattress, and I'd just sit down in the basement playing and playing and playing. And [I] had the drum set down there, [the] piano.

Me and him and Pierre made a great tape. I'll never play it for anybody. Oh my god. He was smashing the drums, and then I would get on the drums, Pierre would get on the bass, and we'd just keep going—it was just amazing. He was a phenomenal drummer back then. He sounded like Billy Cobham. And I showed him some things on the guitar harmonically and showed him some things with his voice, to help him smooth some of his higher notes out. Because he had this really *loud* part of the top

Prince would return home to perform at the annual Northside Summer Fun Festival at the Phyllis Wheatley Community Center even after his career had started taking off. Photograph by Charles Chamblis, circa 1980. Courtesy of the Minnesota Historical Society.

of his register. And I'm like, "You just got to calm that down a bit, you know, tighten up a bit, and it'll ride over your voice." Because we both have really, really high voices. We sounded a lot alike.

Even all these years later, the musicians from The Family are still intensely protective of one another, of Prince, and of their legacy as The Way's house band and the predecessors of his big funk-rock-R&B-new wave explosion. "That's why they called us The Family," Jeff Tresvant says. "We were just there for each other no matter what."

Bassist Sonny Thompson, aka Sonny T., at The New Way in the late '70s. Sonny was an early mentor for Prince and would travel the world with him in his New Power Generation in the 1990s. Photograph by Charles Chamblis. Courtesy of the Minnesota Historical Society.

Chapter Nine

•

PRINCE AND ANDRÉ

See in Chanhassen we ain't scared of police at night
But I didn't always live in Chanhassen
I used to live on Plymouth, Russell, and Penn
Clutching the steering wheel too tight while the helicopter
   circles at night
—PRINCE, freestyling new lyrics to the song "Dreamer" at his
Rally for Peace, Paisley Park, May 2, 2015

LONG BEFORE HE WOULD TOUR THE WORLD alongside Prince as
his first sideman and bassist, and before he would rise to fame
as one of the many bright teenage stars in a new generation of
burgeoning funk-rock musicians from the North Side of Minneapolis, André Cymone was a seventh grader still going by his birthname,
André Anderson. He had just moved with his five siblings out of the
Sumner Housing Projects to a new house on Russell Avenue. It was
the first day of school at Lincoln Junior High, an imposing brick
building that sits in the center of the Near North neighborhood. The
year was 1970, and André Anderson was the new kid in class. Little
did he know that it would also be a day that would dramatically alter
the course of his life—and the Minneapolis music world.

Lincoln Junior High in 1963, the historic site where Prince and André Anderson became fast friends and began their musical partnership. Photograph by Norton & Peel. Courtesy of the Minnesota Historical Society.

"Up against the wall, Anderson," the school's gym teacher, Mr. Lee, said gruffly, handing André a card with his class schedule and gesturing to a far wall of the gymnasium. As André looked around, he realized he didn't know a soul at this new school. The wall was lined with kids, forty or fifty in a row, some clustered together in groups of friends and others lingering there alone. Looking around, André spotted one kid who looked all right. He was short, he was quiet, he had enormous brown eyes, and he had a blossoming Afro hairstyle, just like André.

"Hey, man, how you doing? I'm André," he said, sidling up alongside the quiet kid.

"I'm Prince," the kid replied.

"Prince. Okay. What are you into?" André asked.

"I play music."

"That's interesting. I play music, too."

"Oh," Prince shot back, playing it cool.

Unfazed by the young Prince's deadpan demeanor, André pressed on.

"What do you play?"

"I play piano and guitar," Prince said.

"I play bass and drums, a little guitar," André replied.

Prince raised his eyebrows. "Why don't you come by my dad's house and jam?"

It's a memory that still feels crisp to André, even four decades later. "The rest, as they say, is history," André says, letting out a sigh. More than forty years have passed since that fateful moment, and he is taking a break from sound checking for a show at First Avenue to drive a rented minivan around his old Near North neighborhood, pointing out landmarks from the early days.

Each time we pass a different house or building, a story comes rushing back. "Here it is—this apartment right here is where his dad used to live. Second in, right there," he says. André pulls to the side of the road and looks out the driver's side window, pointing at an apartment complex on the corner of Glenwood Avenue. "We went there and jammed. That was the first time we ever played together. And he was playing *The Man from U.N.C.L.E.* and all that kind of stuff, and the *Peanuts* theme, and I was, like, 'Oh, you can actually play.'"

Prince was living at his dad's studio apartment at the time and occasionally bouncing back and forth between there and his mom's on Eighth Avenue North, where she lived with her new husband. Prince didn't like the looks of his new stepfather, though, and his dad had all the instruments laying around, so it had become his preferred hangout spot. "We said we should start a band together, and he said he had a cousin, Charles, who plays drums. I said I had a sister [Linda] who can play keys, so that was it," André remembers. "We put the band together, and it eventually became Grand Central."

André and Prince gravitated toward one another in a way that felt predestined. As they were jamming that day, André glanced at the photographs that lined the top of the piano belonging to Prince's dad and thought he saw a face that looked eerily familiar. When Prince's dad, John Nelson, got home from work that day, André asked him if he knew the man in the photograph. John looked at André, at the photo on the piano, and back at André again, then cracked up. "You're Fred's son!" It turned out that even though the two young musicians didn't recall knowing each other before, their fathers were musical colleagues, playing in the Prince Rogers Trio. In fact, John remembered that André and Prince had probably played together as kids while waiting for their dads' group to finish performing at the nearby church.

André pulls the van onto the road again and makes his way back up north to show me where he attended junior high. Before we get there, though, he's falling down another rabbit hole of history. "This is the first place we ever played," he says, pointing at a bright blue church building on the corner of Penn and Oak Park Avenues. "Yup, this is the first place we played, right here. It was the People's Church then, but it was also some kind of community center; they used to have all kinds of weird bootleg community situations. We played downstairs. And there was a grocery store right there on that corner. In fact, the money we made, which was only $3—we got $3 apiece—we went right across the street and spent the $3. I don't know if it was symbolic or something, but I bought $3 worth of Mr. Goodbars."

As he continues with the story, we drive north up to Plymouth Avenue, passing by a group of young men who are out canvassing with the community group Neighborhoods Organizing for Change to get residents registered to vote in the upcoming election, which makes André smile. We hook a left and find ourselves heading south down Russell Avenue, the street that many music historians claim is where the Minneapolis Sound was born. That's because André's family, the Andersons, lived at 1244 Russell, and because André's mother, Bernadette, took in a high school–aged Prince and let him crash in her basement, and the boys used to jam in the basement with Linda (Anderson, André's sister) and kids from the neighborhood like Charles Smith, Terry Jackson, William Doughty, and Morris Day. Bernadette Anderson was known as one of the guiding matriarchs of the North Side, spending the majority of her career guiding youth at the YWCA, serving on the boards of community organizations like the Phyllis Wheatley Community Center and KMOJ, and remaining active with the Minneapolis Urban League well into her retirement. Known as Queen Bernie and beloved as a champion of North Side youth, it's no surprise that Bernadette was quick to say yes when André asked if Prince could move in with them (her and her six children) at 1244 Russell. Her open-door policy meant that her house was constantly overflowing with kids from the neighborhood. "We came out of the projects so I grew up always thinking about security," recalled André's brother, Fred Anderson Jr., at a memorial service for Bernadette in 2003. "I am used to people coming to a house, knocking on the door, and waiting to be invited in. So I was surprised to open the door one day and see these kids just walk on in and head to the basement to play music, head to the refrigerator to look for something to eat, and even head to the range and make dinner for themselves."

When André pulls up in front of 1244 Russell, he pauses for a moment in quiet reverence. "That's where it all kinda took place," he says. "It's a little different, because there used to be a big giant Christmas tree there, but it's gone now. In fact that picture that they always show with all of us standing in front of the tree, that was right there." He lingers for a moment longer, as if lost in a sea of memories, then puts the van back in drive and rolls ahead. "So this is the neighborhood."

One of the most striking realizations from André's tour of Near North is just how close together everything sits; you can practically envision a young Morris Day walking over to Terry Jackson's house one afternoon after school to audition for a role in Grand Central, or how easy it would have been for André and Prince to peek in on Sonny Thompson as he practiced bass guitar in his basement and wonder how they were going to upstage him at an upcoming Battle of the Bands show.

As André and Prince's crew were working up their own renditions of the latest songs by Earth, Wind & Fire and the Ohio Players, James Harris III (who would later be known as Jimmy Jam) was gaining steam with his soul project Mind & Matter and would record his album in the basement of a house at 1514 Oliver Avenue North, literally around the corner from where David Hersk cut that first R&B record by the Big M's back in 1958. Meanwhile, Terry Lewis had already established his hard-riding funk band Flyte Tyme (later stylized as *Flyt Tyme*) as a formidable force and was attending classes at North High School with many of the musicians who would come together as the Time.

Looking at all the houses and venues where these bands got their start, it's stunning to see how many musicians of the same age were blossoming out of the same small swath of land. Almost all of the major developments related to that chapter of crystallizing the Minneapolis Sound happened within a mile radius of The Way, and the effects would be felt around the globe. When the highways I-94 and I-394 started snaking their way through the heart of North Minneapolis, it had devastating effects on the area's economy, housing market, and general quality of life. But cutting off Near North from the rest of Minneapolis also had an unintended side effect: it created an incubator for neighborhood youth who were desperate to find a productive way to channel their restless energy.

For those well-versed in the lore of Prince, it's a tale as old as the Time: Prince Rogers Nelson (or Prince Roger Nelson, if you look at his birth certificate) was born to John Nelson and Mattie Shaw on June 7, 1958. Prince spent the first year of his life in South Minneapolis, not far from the hospital where he was born, Mount Sinai. But his parents' origin story was deeply embedded in the streets and community centers of North Minneapolis: his father, a jazz piano player, met his mother, a singer, while playing a concert at the Phyllis Wheatley Community Center. John Nelson's band was called the

A young Prince Rogers Nelson *(front row, left)* with his fifth grade class; and a fifth grader believed by friends and family to be Prince checks out a new listening station at school. Photographs from the John Hay Elementary School yearbook, 1969. Courtesy of Elizabeth Fuller.

Prince Rogers Trio, and John hoped to pass his musical legacy on to his son. So when they welcomed their first child into the world that June, they decided to call him Prince.

John and Mattie moved with baby Prince to Near North on New Year's Eve, 1958, buying a house that sat two blocks south of Plymouth Avenue on Logan. It was in that house that Prince's earliest musical memories would take shape: listening to his father play the piano and sneaking over to bang on the instrument when he wasn't around; hearing stories about his dad's late-night gigs; and listening to records with his younger sister, Tyka.

"Everything was cool until my father left," Prince would tell reporter Barbara Graustark in 1981, during one of the only emotionally revealing on-record interviews of his career. The way Prince told it, his parents separated when he was seven years old. "I was at home living with my mother and my sister, and he had just gone and left his piano. He didn't allow anybody to play it when he was there, because we would just bang on it. So once he left, then I started doing it because nobody else would," he said. "My stepdad came along when I was nine or ten, and I disliked him immediately, because he dealt with a lot of materialistic things. He would bring us a lot of presents all the time, rather than sit down and talk with us or give us companionship. I got real bitter because of that, and I would say all the things that I disliked about him, rather than tell him what I really needed. Which was a mistake, and it kind of hurt our relationship."

It was around this time, when he was nine or ten, that Prince became untethered from anything resembling a predictable life. Not only was he being shuffled between two households, but as the city of Minneapolis grappled with the racial discord that swept the North Side in the summer of 1967, Prince would be one of the first children to start participating in an intercity busing program, leaving the boundaries of the segregated Near North neighborhood to ride past the manicured lawns of Bryn Mawr and the mansions that surround Lake of the Isles. This was quite the feat for a young African American kid from North: although the neighborhood was starkly separated from its surrounding communities, Prince started floating outside the boundary lines almost immediately. "I'm as much a part of the city where I grew up as I am anything. I was very lucky to be born here, because I saw both sides of the racial issue, the oppression and the equality," Prince told *Minnesota Monthly* in 1997. "I got the best of all worlds here. I saw what happens here, and it's not like what happens in, say, Atlanta. I used to be part of a busing program that took me through Kenwood every day. You can check it out in the song 'The Sacrifice of Victor.' That runs down the whole scene here."

As with that candid interview from the early period of his career, Prince's song "The Sacrifice of Victor," released on 1992's *Love Symbol Album,* was one of the most explicitly autobiographical and revealing songs he would ever release. With a callout to "Sonny, please"—

a reference to his childhood friend and the New Power Generation bassist who plays on the track, Sonny Thompson—Prince lays it out over a bristling funk beat peppered with horn blasts:

> 1967 in a bus marked public schools
> Rode me and a group of unsuspecting political tools
> Our parents wondered what it was like to have another color near
> So they put their babies together to eliminate the fear

In the same song, Prince also calls back to the unrest of the late 1960s, singing "Dr. King was killed and the streets / They started burnin'," but it's unclear how aware he and his classmates would have been of the grocery stores that burned or the National Guard troops that briefly occupied their neighborhood. Prince would have been eight when the first unrest broke out in August 1966 and nine when the fires were lit in 1967. Also, the assassination of Dr. Martin Luther King Jr. wouldn't take place until April 1968, so it's possible he was reflecting on rioting he saw on TV rather than in his own city.

Prince would bounce back to the schools in his own neighborhood long enough to finish out elementary school at John Hay and meet André Anderson on that fateful first day at the neighboring Lincoln Junior High. But before long, his educational experience would be thrown into chaos again. The intercity busing program had regained steam after a particularly harsh report on segregation in St. Paul and Minneapolis Public Schools that was released by the State Human Rights Department. In an effort to stem the "increasing separation of minority-group children from their white peers," the state mandated that the schools step up their efforts starting in the 1970–71 school year, which meant that instead of finishing out his pivotal junior high years with his new best friend and bandmates, he would be bused down to South Minneapolis to attend Bryant Junior High.

At Bryant, Prince would play on the basketball team with his half-brother, Duane Nelson, and would cross paths for the first time with James Harris III (aka Jimmy Jam), who grew up on the South Side. And it was where he would contemplate the inner workings of the entertainment industry for the first time, taking two years of music theory and business of music classes from Bryant Junior High teacher Jimmy Hamilton, and showing up for school an hour early each day to jam on various instruments in his classroom.

To think of a young Prince floating adrift in this between space, his home life crumbling, staring out the windows of a city passing him by, it's easy to understand how he slowly detached from the day-to-day concerns that plague most teenagers and wandered into a musically obsessed dream state. To imagine him shuffling from home to home, school to school, neighborhood to neighborhood, it's no wonder that even his earliest musical explorations couldn't be bound by genre or rules.

While it's tempting to cite Prince's life story as a monologue, however, it's common knowledge that he was one of the many kids his age who utilized the teen centers and educational facilities that sprang up in the wake of the 1966 and 1967 unrest—and that his time connecting with his musical peers would help steer him toward the pop superstardom he would soon embrace.

Another member of Grand Central, Terry Jackson, fondly remembers those earliest days of Prince's musical life. Like Prince, Terry was beholden to the city's intercity busing program and shuffled from Kenwood Elementary School to John Hay at the same time as Prince. Though they wouldn't collaborate for several years, he recalls a third-grade Prince making his debut on piano at the school's talent show:

I remember watching him at least twice growing up in a couple talent shows at John Hay. I remember seeing him do a tap dance. He was out there tap dancing. And then one talent show he played [the theme from] *Batman* on the piano, and *The Man from U.N.C.L.E.*, too. That was another popular show back then. . . . He did a couple talent shows by himself. And years later it was him as a trio with his cousin Charles—we called him Chazz—and André. That was about the time we were in Lincoln Junior High School.

Terry Jackson lived next door to the Andersons, so by the time seventh grade drew to a close, he hadn't only become the latest member of Grand Central: his basement had become another rehearsal space for the growing band. "I'm an only child, I had a big house right next door to André Cymone's crib, and my mom was cool," says Jackson. "So I said, 'We're gonna do it over here.' So they came over to my house and started rehearsing at my house. I didn't have any instruments. My mother went to a pawnshop and got me a conga drum at a pawnshop, so I started playing congas in seventh grade. One of my auntie's boyfriends had a Santana album that I just fell in love with, and I got into all this Latin stuff."

In those earliest days, the band went through a couple of name changes before ultimately settling on Grand Central. As Jackson recalls it, they played at least one talent show at North High School billed as Phoenix, inspired by the Three Dog Night song "Flight of the Phoenix," but it didn't stick. "Then we wanted to name ourselves Sex Machine," he recalls, laughing. "There was a song by James Brown called 'Sex Machine,' and a song by Sly and the Family Stone called 'Sex Machine,' and our mothers didn't like that one bit. So that was out the window. No, we're not being called Sex Machine, that's not happening, not at twelve and thirteen years old. We're not getting that name." Prince eventually suggested Grand Central, a combination of one of his favorite bands at the time, Grand Funk Railroad, and his high school, Central.

The band was cobbling together instruments and equipment at that point, borrowing basses and drum sets from friends, and soon realized they needed some kind of support. They were recruited by a local manager, Frank Jackson, to open for an older South Minneapolis teen band called Brainstorm and share the group's equipment. Before too long, they had earned enough of a reputation that Jackson was booking them to headline their own gigs at community centers around the city. "Now we were kids," Terry Jackson says. "Essentially, our mothers were our guardians and our managers and our roadies and all that stuff. My mom had a station wagon, so that became our road car for gigs. She did a lot of that. She helped us out

Grand Central's André Anderson *(foreground)* and key-boardist Linda Anderson play the Minneapolis Central High School prom in 1976. Photograph from the 1976 *Centralian* yearbook. Courtesy of the Hennepin County Library Yearbook Collection.

a lot. So we ended up getting all this new equipment, being managed by Frank Jackson at the time, and started playing in little corner bars and schools and school gigs, community center gigs, and stuff of that nature."

André recalls that his mother, Bernadette, would often take charge of the group and help them find gigs, too. "I mean, we played at the State Fair, we played everywhere," he says. "My mom would have us playing anywhere. We'd play in the backyard. She'd have a bunch of friends over for card parties; we'd play. So if you can imagine—because, you know, Prince became a very big superstar—but [back

The historic Grand Central band, featuring *(left to right)* Linda Anderson, André "Cymone" Anderson, Morris Day, Terry Jackson, Prince, and William "Hollywood" Doughty, in the front yard of the Anderson home at 1244 Russell Avenue North in Minneapolis. Courtesy of André Cymone.

then] my mom would just say, 'I don't care what you guys are doing, you guys are going to have to come down to the Elks, and we need a band, so you guys are going to play.'"

Back then there were endless gigs for young bands willing to play covers of the latest rock, funk, and pop hits, especially at the local schools. This was long before a time when a DJ could plug in an iPod to get the kids dancing; the schools relied mostly on live music for all of their homecomings, winter formals, and proms. "I remember one gig in particular was really the most hilarious thing because we were late—I mean, we were, like, really late—and they had hired us to do the prom thing," recalls André. "We were late, and they were waiting outside. Because back then, they couldn't just play records. People didn't want to just hear that; there wasn't a DJ thing. Back then, they wanted live music. When we finally got there, we played, and it was a great, great show, and they really loved it and appreciated it."

As the band's demand grew, they expanded their lineup as well. In addition to Terry on percussion, Chazz on drums, André on bass, Prince on guitar, and André's sister, Linda Anderson, on the Farfisa organ, the group added William Doughty, who now goes by the name Hollywood, to flesh out the more Latin-inspired percussion elements of their evolving sound. "Maybe by ninth, tenth grade, we were that band. We were whole," Terry says.

It was around this time that Morris Day recalls first discovering and falling in love with the group. "I saw this band play, and they were incredible—you know, like fourteen- or fifteen-year-old kids, puttin' it down like adults," he remembers. "And I was just amazed. It was just the kind of thing that I wanted to be involved with." Morris approached André and complimented him on the band, and pretty soon he had figured out a way to show André what he could do behind a drumkit. As he recalls:

One time we skipped school, we went over to my house, and I had my drums set up in my room in front of a huge speaker, about five feet tall. I blasted some Tower of Power, and I got on the drums and started clicking some [David] Garibaldi, and I stopped, and André was looking at me. He's like, "Man, I didn't know you could play like that." He's like, "Man, we gotta talk. We've been having a little trouble with our drummer." So I brought my drums by one day—they were practicing at the timbale player Terry Jackson's basement at the time—and everybody heard me play, and that was it. I never broke my drums down. Moved Charles's drums outta the way—sorry, Charles—and there mine stayed.

Terry Jackson remembers being impressed by Day's playing: "A lot of people don't know Morris played drums. He was a very superior drummer . . . so we started doing more sophisticated stuff. There was an artist named Eumir Deodato, and he had this song called 'Super Strut.' It was a complicated instrumental that we just practiced and practiced. We had it so syncopated that Morris would start on rolling his drums, then Hollywood started rolling on his drums, and I started rolling—we made it a tight pattern of three different drums."

If there is one pattern that emerges out of every story about these high school bands on the North Side in the 1970s, it's that they all practiced like crazy. Day and night, night and day, nestled into the basements of houses on the north and south sides of Plymouth Avenue, brewing up concoctions that would be unleashed at the next dance or community center battle. Jackson estimates that rehearsals at his house would stretch anywhere from four to six hours, happening nearly every day of the week. Whereas the Anderson household was crowded with siblings and their honorary brother, Prince, Terry's basement had more room for the band to spread out and jam. He remembers those subterranean sessions, and one outdoor jam in particular:

The basement was finished—it had a bar that was built in. It had paneled walls and everything. Very large area. Large enough for us to rehearse on one side have a ping-pong table on the other side. My dad had this routine where when he was tired of us, he'd just be at the top of the stairs and he'd flick the lights. No matter what we were doing down there, the lights started flickering, it's time to shut everything off. And after we'd moved up in equipment, André got this Traynor bass amp. It was huge—about this tall and about that wide [holding his arms out wide]. My dad would come downstairs and say, "You guys are shaking the pictures off the walls." That's how much vibration we were causing in the house and stuff.

So one summer day we decided to take it all upstairs, sit on the patio, and rehearse, because it was a nice day out. We started on the patio, and we're rehearsing and everything, and because it was the second house from the corner and so it was real close to one of the main streets, people started trickling in down the alley and coming in the backyard. Before you knew it, the whole backyard was full, the alley was full. There were people spilling out into the street from back, hearing us rehearse. The police had to come and stop us. Police came and stopped the whole thing and said we were causing a public nuisance or whatever. The police actually stopped us from rehearsing because there were too many people stacked up through the alleys and street during this rehearsal. That was a cool memory about being at the house.

So what did Grand Central sound like? That's a question that remains on Prince scholars' minds to this day, thanks to the fact that no recordings of the group have ever been released (though they do exist). Like so many aspects of oral histories, the sound of Grand Central is something that exists only in the collective memories of the people who saw them perform or were alongside Prince onstage; for an artist whose recordings and live shows have since been obsessively documented and archived, Prince's time in his first band remains blissfully vague, funky, and impressionistic.

"What we sounded like? I guess we sounded like a lot of the bands of the time, like Earth, Wind & Fire," says André. He goes on:

We did a lot of rock 'n' roll, like Grand Funk Railroad. And Chicago. We did a lot of funk, Ohio Players; we did some Jimi Hendrix. And I think that had a lot to do with our music, and what they call the Minneapolis Sound. Growing up in Minneapolis, the radio was amazing, because at the time they just played really good rock. They didn't play very much R&B at all, you know; KMOJ, you could hardly get that. But they played really amazing rock 'n' roll. I mean, at the time, we were broke, so it wasn't like you could run out and get records at will, so when you heard it, you'd literally record it off the radio. Different reality.

André recalls spending hours listening to the progressive rock station KQRS, gleaning inspiration off their free-form playlist of heady rock tunes. Although it's now regarded as a tightly programmed classic-rock station that respins the same few Top 40 hits from the Rolling Stones, Tom Petty, and Fleetwood Mac, back then it wasn't uncommon to hear a DJ play an entire new album from start to finish or mix together deep cuts from exploratory prog-rock artists like Yes, Frank Zappa, Pink Floyd, King Crimson, and one of Grand Central's idols, Carlos Santana. "The old KQ after midnight, that was the bomb station," Prince told *Minnesota Monthly* in 1997. "I'd stay up all night listening to it. That's where I discovered Carlos Santana, Maria Muldaur, and Joni Mitchell. Was I influenced by that? Sure I was. Back then I always tried to play like Carlos, or Boz Scaggs."

It was in this particular period of their trajectory where the overwhelming whiteness of the Twin Cities would actually work in Prince's favor. Although their roots were buried deep in the black jazz community of North Minneapolis, with their lineage connecting them to jazz groups like the Prince Rogers Trio and Bobby Lyle and R&B idol Maurice McKinnies, Prince and André didn't listen to much modern-day R&B and funk music, mostly because they literally couldn't get it. The city's black community radio stations, first KUXL and then KMOJ, would only reach certain areas of North Minneapolis, and their increasing mobility due to school busing and wider-spread gigs meant that they were spending less and less time tethered to their immediate community and more time engaging with the majority population and pop culture of the city. Grand Central's embrace of white rock music would become a defining characteristic of what is now referred to as the Minneapolis Sound. They weren't bound by styles of music, neighborhoods, or ethnicities; they found liberation in the simple act of making music they loved and channeling the artists they admired, regardless of labels or genres.

"That's one of the things about Minnesota radio that had a lot to do with the sound that a lot of us called the 'Minneapolis Sound,' from a musician's standpoint, because there was a lot of rock on the radio, and you did listen to it when you were in your car. You did listen to a lot of very album-oriented, rock-oriented music. And there's no way it's not going to permeate and work its way into what you were trying do," André says.

* * *

A photograph of a fashion show also manages to capture an early public performance by Grand Central, with Prince on organ, André Cymone on bass, and Morris Day on drums. Photograph by Charles Chamblis. Courtesy of the Minnesota Historical Society.

By the end of high school, Grand Central had become a dominating force in the Minneapolis teen band scene. In addition to their obvious natural talent, Terry Jackson credits a lot of Grand Central's success to the underlying competitive spirit that seemed to push and pull the bands of his era together. "We were all athletic at the time back then, and with a lot of the school dances being on Friday nights, we couldn't participate in the sports—because you could either do the dance or do the sports. So the music became our sport, basically. That became our competition. Instead of battling on base-ball fields or basketball fields or football fields, we were battling on-stage against other bands."

"Back then, everybody was in a band," adds André. "If you weren't in a band back then, you kind of weren't cool."

"We ended up having a really big playlist," says Terry. "I would say we had a good, maybe two to three hundred songs altogether, by the time it was all said and done, through the years. Like I said, from seventh grade to twelfth grade, so pretty much six years of that experience of doing that with those guys. But it was a strive for each of us to do something better than the next person. It was a competitive spirit and stuff that really put Prince on the precipice where he is today. We would go and study other bands and listen to them. We wouldn't go just to listen or hang out. We would go to study it. 'How are you playing that? How are you doing this?'"

The hours of rehearsals and competitions paid off. By the time Grand Central was ready to call it quits in 1976, André says it was clear to the elders in their community that the musicians were going to go on to do something professionally as adults. They just weren't sure what that would look like yet:

People went crazy when we were kids. Oddly enough, you wouldn't think—just for a local thing—but it was pretty clear to most people that saw us play, that we were eventually gonna do something. People would say it all the time. I would say it because I was always bragging: "We're the best band, period." I was a bigmouth back then. I've become a lot more humble, but I used to be the band bigmouth, so I would start a lot of stuff. I would tell other bands that they couldn't play, just to get them to let us play. I said, "We can play better than you guys. You guys ain't—you can't play—you don't know how to play. You guys ain't shit." And finally I'd just keep going until they'd say, "Let me hear you play."

André pauses, smirking mischievously. "Then we'd go up and steal the gig."

Chapter Ten

•

FUNKYTOWN

2 get paid in the Moneyapple, got 2 be bold.
—PRINCE, "Northside"

N THE 1960S, the African American community of the Twin Cities, especially those who had been displaced from Rondo and sections of North Minneapolis, had trouble seeing I-94 as little more than a four-lane, blazing-hot concrete symbol of how inconsequential their well-being and community seemed to the larger Minnesota population and government leaders. But by the '70s, a younger generation of artists and creative hopefuls were beginning to see it as something else: Interstate 94 was a way out of town.

It is poignant that one of the first bands to capture some of Prince's guitar work on tape, when they recruited him as a session player in 1976, was called 94 East. For young artists who dreamed of something larger than what the Land of Sky Blue Waters could offer them, 94 East was the pathway out of Minneapolis, through the heart of St. Paul, across the open prairies of the Midwest and on toward New York, a city that seemed to pulse with possibility. The dream of New York had come alive in the heart of Prince as he graduated from Central High School and set his sights on establishing himself in the larger music industry. Prince was no longer content

After Prince left Grand Central to focus on his solo debut for Warner Bros., the band continued as Champagne. Pictured are *(left to right)* Morris Day, William "Hollywood" Doughty, Linda Anderson, and André Anderson. Photograph by Charles Chamblis. Courtesy of the Minnesota Historical Society.

to merely dominate high school dances, battles of the bands, and block parties at his neighborhood's community centers. He wanted to hear his records played on Top 40 radio.

Pretty much everything that Prince did that summer made it clear that he was hell-bent on getting to the Big Apple. He knew there were studios there, and one of his older half-sisters was living there already. "I think it is very hard for a band to make it in this state, even if they're good. Mainly because there aren't any big record companies or studios in this state," Prince would tell his high school newspaper, *The Centralian,* a few months before graduation. "I really feel that if we would have lived in Los Angeles or New York or some other big city, we would have gotten over by now."

Grand Central would disband shortly after Prince spoke to his school's newspaper, and a new version of the band billed as Champagne (variably spelled as Shampayne) would continue with Linda Anderson and Morris Day leading the charge. André would stay with Champagne for a while, observing Prince's movements from a close distance as the two still resided together at the Andersons' house, and the two friends would experiment for a while with making music without one another.

Prince fell in with his metaphorical big brothers in The Family, spending long hours jamming with Sonny Thompson and talking his way into the studio for a recording session at Sound 80, where he would earn a decent wage playing guitar on their song "Got to Be Something Here." As Thompson recalls about this period: "Prince, he joined our band for a while. He was with Grand Central, and I don't know what happened, they got in some kind of food fight or something, and our guitar player, he acted a fool, he didn't want to play guitar, so it's like, well, why don't we just get Prince? He ain't playing with nobody. We talked to Prince, and he was like, 'Well, I'm trying to get to New York.' So he played with us for a minute, and recorded on this song that I wrote; he played guitar and sang background on it."

"Sonny's singing lead vocals, and [Prince is] singing background vocals and doing lead guitar," adds Pierre Lewis, who would cover the cost of the band's studio time that day and leave the session with control of the master tapes. The Family ended up disbanding not long after their session, so Pierre wouldn't release the song until 1978, when he included it as a bonus track on an album by his group the Lewis Connection. To this day, original pressings of the album remain incredibly sought-after by collectors, and a reissue of *The Lewis Connection* on Numero Group in 2013 introduced the historic song to a new generation of scholars.

Listening back to the recording years later, one might expect a hard-driving tune reminiscent of the band's favorite funk and progressive rock bands of the era. But instead, "Got to Be Something Here" is quite tender and sweet; Sonny Thompson's falsetto blends so seamlessly with Prince's high-register harmonies that their voices are practically indistinguishable, and Pierre Lewis's woozy, crooning organ melodies sound like a very subdued, polite spacecraft requesting transmission to another world. The guitar part is equally subtle, mostly strumming along to the beat of the soft ballad, a far cry from the blistering solos and technical pyrotechnics that would define Prince's creative aesthetic. If any single element of "Got to Be Something Here" connects the band to Prince's soon-to-explode solo career, it's the synthesized strings and piano chords played toward the end of the song by Pierre Lewis—Prince would borrow that same synthesizer and keep it for several months, using it to record the songs on his solo debut, *For You*, like "Soft and Wet."

"Prince didn't have any equipment at all," Lewis says. "So he was borrowing a guitar from Sonny, and he was borrowing a synthesizer from me to do the keyboard parts on his demo and on his first album. He was playing with Grand Central, but when he quit they said he couldn't have the equipment, because it was owned by the band, so he couldn't take nothing with him." As soon as he set foot in the Sound 80 studios for that first session with The Family, Prince would start accumulating not just the instruments he needed but the industry connections that would help him shape his sound and image as a solo artist.

The Sound 80 session that produced "Got to Be Something Here" was helmed by David Rivkin, who had already been working for years with the local company ASI. It was the first of many instances in the

Prince at the piano in Chris Moon's Uptown-based Moon Sound Studios, where he recorded demos for his debut album, *For You*. Photograph by Larry Falk. Courtesy of the photographer.

You'll be bug-eyed —— at how great this can make you sound

NEW
SOUND 80
ALL SOLID-STATE
RECORDING CONSOLE

NEW
SOUND 80
SCULLY
16-TRACK RECORDER

SOUND 80 will give you the fattest sound you can get with the new 16-track

A 4-hour 16-track session any time of the day or night for only $380 (plus tape)

EQUIPMENT: Scully 16-8-4-2 and mono recorders; 4 Stereo EMT echo chambers; Moog Synthesizer; all new, solid state 44-position recording console; 16-position equalization; high and low pass cut-off filtering; limiting, compression and ring modulation.

Come out to see and hear for yourself

SOUND 80 INC

An advertisement for Sound 80 studios in South Minneapolis brags about its state-of-the-art equipment and the "fattest sound you can get." By the end of the 1970s, the studio had been used by both Bob Dylan and Prince. Originally published in *Insider* magazine, May 1970.

coming years when Prince would create music in close proximity to at least one of St. Louis Park's famous Rivkin brothers. By the end of the year, Prince would also be introduced to Bobby Rivkin, whom he would rename Bobby Z and recruit as the drummer for his band the Revolution. As Bobby Z recalls it, Prince walked through those doors at Sound 80 at just the right time. "There was a lot of knowledge about how to make records, and people were really learning the craft of what it would take to get an artist from Minneapolis off the ground," he says, citing his brother's previous success capturing hit records by rock bands like the Chancellors, the Castaways, and the High Spirits at Kay Bank Studios for the Soma label.

Bob Dylan had just visited Sound 80 in '75 to re-record tracks for his critically acclaimed album *Blood on the Tracks*, and the success of that album and the fact that Cat Stevens had just utilized the space added to the studio's allure. Although he was young and inexperienced at the time, Prince would record his first demos at Sound 80 with David Rivkin during the studio's heyday. And he would take the money he earned recording with The Family to hop a plane to New York, tape in hand, to attempt his grand entrance into the larger music industry.

Back home in Minneapolis, the engineer Chris Moon of Moon Sound Studios in Uptown Minneapolis had gotten his hands on Prince's demo tape and figured he had a hit on his hands. Moon decided to take the tape to a young ad man, Owen Husney, who had come up in a successful R&B garage band, the High Spirits, and was starting to dip his toes back into the music industry. "Right in this window right here, if you had a time machine and looked in there, you would see a young Chris Moon waiting in that office to meet me with a demo tape he made with Prince," Husney recalls with a wistful sigh, peering into the window of his old office at 430 Oak Grove Street in Loring Park, Minneapolis, in 2017. "I had heard enough stories about people who thought they had the next greatest thing, and so I wouldn't see him. Finally, when I let him into my office, Chris put the tape on and I was just mesmerized.... These guys ... weren't just emulating the sound of the day: what I heard was people going for another sound." All at once, the flood of several instruments and a silky smooth and emotionally fraught falsetto voice filled his office, each piece of the song perfectly intertwined.

"Who is this group?" Husney asked.

"It's not a group," Moon replied. "It's mostly one kid, singing, writing, all the instruments."

Husney's curiosity was officially piqued. Ironically, Prince was in New York at this point, crashing with his sister and attempting to shop himself around to various labels. Moon and Husney called him up and told him to come back home: this story was going to get its start in Minneapolis. Husney started hustling up meetings with all the major labels, landing meetings with Columbia Records, A&M, and Warner Bros., all the while inviting Prince to jam in his office after hours and observing him back at work in Moon Sound Studios, where he was continuing to record demos and master techniques like multitrack recording. When he'd landed back home in Minneapolis, Prince would also reconnect with Pepé Willie, a struggling musician whom Prince had long admired since the two had met while Pepé was dating one of his older cousins. Prince would get hired as a session musician once again, laying down guitar parts with Pepé and his old friend André Cymone for a series of 1977 recordings that would be issued after Prince's rise to fame as 94 East's *Minneapolis Genius*.

While Husney worked on developing the business side of his career, Prince became singularly focused on his music. It's a period that many consider Prince's most formative as he transitioned into a fully formed and increasingly complex solo artist. He was logging wildly long hours in the studio, tinkering around for ten or more hours at a time, and rehearsing for equally long stretches with collaborators like André Cymone, dreaming up new melodies and sounds.

It was around this time that Bobby Z first met Prince, in yet another association that felt predestined; Bobby was working both as a session drummer for Moon Sound and as a runner for Owen Husney's advertising and marketing firm. "I kind of lit the candle at both ends," Bobby says. "My job was to be part of the experience day and night, let's just say. I saw him in the studio, walked by the door, and heard a whiff of music that changed my life forever." Bobby recalls being instantly impressed with Prince's abilities, not just as a technically proficient player on several different instruments but as a budding studio engineer. As soon as he inked his deal with Warner Bros., Prince told the label that he would be producing his own albums, which was received with a heavy dose of skepticism and dismay. In a grand sense of foreshadowing, Prince would pen a song for the label to celebrate their new contract, titled "I Hope We Work It Out."

For those like Bobby watching Prince up close in rehearsals, there was no question that he would be capable of handling himself in the studio. "The vocals were already multitracked at this point, and [when] first hearing his self-harmonies, which we all know now are amazing—there was just a feeling in there. And then watching him play piano, I saw the piano moving. I'd never seen anybody's hands play a piano like that, and hear what I'm hearing. The way he would rhythmically play, you could just tell this was something beyond playing the notes or anticipating the notes; there was more to it than that. It just had an unbelievable vibe."

By this point Prince had moved to South Minneapolis, not far from the Uptown neighborhood he would crystallize in song, and was setting up camp in Pepé Willie's basement to jam out his songs with the members of his new and evolving live band. "That's where they'd practice, from about ten o'clock in the morning to ten o'clock at night, every single day," Pepé told *Rolling Stone* in 2016.

Nearly everyone who was around Prince in those early years of his solo career recall their memories with a sense of starry-eyed wonder. But it wasn't all diamonds and pearls for the newest artist on the Warner Bros. label. Prince would still need to struggle through a few years of uncertainty, nerve-wracking performances, and industry politics before breaking through to the mainstream success he knew he deserved.

While Prince was busy traveling to San Francisco to record his debut album, *For You,* and woodshedding with his band, many of his classmates and friendly rivals were also gaining steam with their post–high school projects. Although they had first met in their early teens and had been facing off in battles of the bands showcases for years in their groups Mind & Matter and Flyte Tyme, it wasn't until the late 1970s that James "Jimmy Jam" Harris III and Terry Lewis would finally cement a partnership that would carry them through the next several decades.

Jimmy Jam met Terry Lewis for the first time when he was thirteen years old, and the pair was participating in a summer school program called Upward Bound at the University of Minnesota, where older students would tutor younger learners about basic skills like math. Terry Lewis was three years older than Jimmy and seemed instantly cool to him: he recalls walking past Terry's dorm room where the students were housed for the summer and watching him play bass along with a record by Kool & The Gang. "I said to myself, 'Who is this dude?' I was instantly attracted to him. I thought he was just so cool. He was the older brother I didn't have," he told *Wax Poetics.*

Terry Lewis *(center)* and his band Flyt Tyme, which evolved to include Garry "Jellybean" Johnson on drums and Cynthia Johnson on vocals. Photograph by Charles Chamblis. Courtesy of Minnesota Historical Society.

Even though he was still in junior high, Jimmy had already started picking up gigs around town playing the drums with his father, the jazz pianist Cornbread Harris, and he would impress Terry one day in the school's lunchroom when the older musician caught him tinkering around on the piano. Terry was assembling his first band and had already recruited drummer Garry "Jellybean" Johnson and saxophonist David "Batman" Eiland to come perform with him for an end-of-summer event for Upward Bound. Although Jimmy considered himself more of a drummer at that point, Terry convinced him to borrow his dad's keyboards and join the band for their first performance before going their separate ways at program's end.

Jimmy and Terry remained friends but also stoked a growing rivalry. Jimmy Jam had joined another band of older musicians called Mind & Matter and was focusing his energy on creating soulful, soothing ballads and harmonic dance songs in the vein of his

As Flyt Tyme (later stylized as Flyte Tyme and Flyte Time) grew in size, its parties got wilder. Here, members are decked out in surreal, Parliament Funkadelic–inspired Halloween costumes for a holiday party. Photograph by Charles Chamblis. Courtesy of the Minnesota Historical Society.

producer idols out of Philadelphia, Gamble & Huff (Kenneth Gamble and Leon A. Huff), who were writing hits for the O'Jays and Harold Melvin & the Blue Notes. Terry, on the other hand, was more interested in creating deeply grooving, futuristic-sounding funk music in the vein of Parliament Funkadelic. Although they wouldn't realize it at the time, the fact that they were interested in such wildly different yet complementary styles of music connected to the lineage of popular black music would eventually work to their favor: if one of the defining characteristics of the Minneapolis Sound is its aggressive blend of genres, it might have actually helped Jimmy and Terry's dynamic that they took the time to hone their own sounds before teaming up to make something together.

By the late '70s, Mind & Matter had logged hours recording demos in a basement studio in Near North and Jimmy Jam had started honing his skills as a DJ, while Flyte Tyme had become a hot commodity in the club scene. In that era, the cool hangouts for seeing live funk and R&B music were the Nacirema Club (which was *American* spelled backwards) in South Minneapolis off Fourth Avenue and Thirty-eighth Street, which was basically an old duplex that had been turned into an underground basement venue, and the colorful and intimate Cozy Bar in North.

It was at the Nacirema that Flyte Tyme would score gigs warming up the stage for Wee Willie Walker when he was holding it down every weekend with his house band, Solid on Down, which also featured The Family's Joe Lewis on drums. And it was at the Nacirema where Prince would stop down between stints in the recording studio to observe the players and occasionally sit in. "He used to come to the Nacirema every Sunday where I was and come up and play with me," Walker recalls. "He'd come and sit at my table and never say a word. Never say a word. And then he'd say, 'Mind if I play?' When he went up and played, everything sounded better. That was easy to recognize."

By the time they were opening for Willie Walker at the Nacirema, Flyte Tyme had solidified its lineup to include the rising star Cynthia Johnson on lead vocals, a gospel singer who quickly became

Prince

I N   CONCERT

A Benefit Performance for the Capri Theatre

Friday, January 5, 8:00 pm

$4.00 in advance $4.75 at the door

Capri Theatre, 2027 West Broadway

PRINCE

A ticket stub for the first big hometown show by post–Grand Central Prince at the Capri Theatre in North Minneapolis. Prince had just released his debut album, *For You,* on Warner Bros. in April 1978, and he recruited André Cymone, Dez Dickerson, Matt "Dr." Fink, Gayle Chapman, and Bobby Z (Rivkin) to fill out his live band. Courtesy of the Minnesota Historical Society.

an impressive newcomer on the funk scene; Jellybean Johnson on drums; David Eiland on saxophone; Anton "Tony" Johnson on guitar; and Terry Lewis on bass; with a variety of additional players cycling in to amp up the horn section. By the late '70s, Cynthia Johnson had become such a revered singer that she showed up on the radar of an up-and-coming producer in town by the name of Steven Greenberg, who was logging hours at Sound 80 recording with David Rivkin to create his new studio project called Lipps, Inc. "The Lipps, Inc., group was just me in the beginning," Greenberg recalls. "I ran a mobile disco system, I was a DJ at parties and weddings, etc., and I figured I could write one of these songs, one of these disco songs. So I wrote lots of songs at the time, and 'Funkytown' was one of them. And it ended up being a good one." In hindsight, that seems quite an understatement, considering the lasting impact "Funkytown" has had on pop culture and dance music charts. To this day, it remains one of the best-selling songs to ever come out of Minnesota and has

Steven Greenberg *(left)*, Cynthia Johnson, and drummer Bobby Vandell of Lipps, Inc., at their debut live show at Duffy's following the release of "Funkytown." Johnson would grab a suitcase and wave it around onstage as she sang "Gotta make a move to a town that's right for me." Courtesy of Steven Greenberg.

been featured in countless television shows, movies, commercials, and video games, not to mention blasted on dance floors for three decades and counting.

But back in 1979, "Funkytown" was one of a batch of songs Steven Greenberg had written to share with his new label, Casablanca Records. And although it would soon become the pride of Minneapolis, Greenberg actually wrote it about hoping to leave his hometown for somewhere cooler, searching for a scene that was more culturally integrated and diverse. "Well, the lyrics are 'Gotta make a move to a town that's right for me,' basically, and I wanted to get out of here," he says. "The scene here was very bland, there was no black radio. Maybe KMOJ played a little bit, but it wasn't really out there, and I grew up on the Temptations and Motown and stuff like that, Earth, Wind & Fire, and you couldn't get that here. It was very vanilla. A very vanilla market."

Greenberg started asking around about finding a soulful singer who could tackle the hooks on his songs "Rocket" and "Funkytown," and on the advice of the respected vocalists Sue Ann Carwell and Patty Peterson, he was told he should call up a rising star named Cynthia Johnson. "Kind of a weird deal, just calling some woman out of the blue and saying, 'I wrote this song, would you sing it?' Anyway, we ended up partnering up, and Cynthia and I then became Lipps, Inc.," he recalls. "Before that, during that time it was kind of a producer's medium, and producers would make a record and hire singers to sing, but finally I found a partner in Cynthia, and I'm certainly glad I did."

Johnson recorded her vocal parts toward the end of 1979, and the song debuted in January 1980, its synthesized and giddy dance beat capitalizing on the last gasp of the disco fad that had consumed the pop music world in the '70s. Greenberg describes its debut:

> After it came out it took a major move on the dance charts—I think they were still called the disco charts back then—from, like, 66 to 10. And then they told me that it had sold twenty-three thousand copies in New York in one day. And I said, "Is that good?" And they laughed. They were like, "Oh, god, is that good? Greenberg, get with it! It's incredible! New York, one day, twenty-three thousand!" And so that's when I realized that something was going on.

Before he knew it, "Funkytown" had crossed over from the dance charts to the Top 40, and Greenberg was being shuttled around Los Angeles in a white stretch limo, toasting his success at high-profile meetings and parties. And back home, folks in the scene were scratching their heads at what seemed to be a total anomaly: a producer who had meticulously crafted a piece of music in the studio and was mostly disconnected from the bubbling underground R&B scene, or the thundering punk and new wave uprising that would explode out of 7th St Entry in the early '80s.

Even though "Funkytown" was recorded by a hometown artist, the local radio market was the last to pick it up. "Twin Cities radio stations . . . have seemed prejudiced against 'Funkytown' because of its success on the disco and soul charts," Jon Bream wrote in the *Star Tribune* in June 1980. But suddenly, even the vanilla market that Greenberg was railing against in the song had embraced "Funkytown." First it was on KSTP, then KDWB, then it was everywhere.

But what happened to the eighteen-year-old studio whiz who could play every instrument, was signed to Warner Bros., and was supposed to be the next big thing? And how did this relatively unknown artist end up beating him to the top of the charts? Owen Husney remembered this period of Prince's trajectory vividly, in an interview for the documentary *Prince Unauthorized* in 1992:

> After the first album came out and just did so-so, here we are sitting around licking our wounds . . . and then bang, we're sitting there, and this record "Funkytown" comes out. By this young white kid from Minneapolis. And all of a sudden we're looking at the charts and we said, "Wait a minute. This other record from this young white kid just went #1 on the black charts and the urban charts?" Then it went #1 on the pop charts. Then it went #1 on the dance charts. Then it goes #1 in every free country on earth.
>
> I don't know if Prince will ever cop to this, but I think that record served to propel him. I know it caught him. It had to. I think that that served to propel him on to really do what he had to do.

Whereas Steven Greenberg sought to escape the lily-white vanilla market in Minneapolis—and did so by capitalizing on a black woman's vocal prowess—Prince had chosen to stay rooted in Minneapolis and bring his outsider funkiness to the inner city. But after seeing his first singles relegated to the black music charts and watching his friends continue to struggle to play gigs outside of the Chitlin' Circuit of black bars and underground spots in the Twin Cities, he was starting to become frustrated with the racism that was holding him back from reaching his full potential. And so he did what he knew how to do best: he rehearsed relentlessly, he crafted sharper

A late-era incarnation of The Family band included brothers Randy and Mikel Barber on guitar, Joe Lewis on drums, Sonny Thompson on bass, and Chico Smith on saxophone. In this photograph from 1980 they are performing in the just-opened 7th St Entry at Sam's, soon to be known as First Avenue. Photograph copyright Steven Laboe.

hooks and tighter songs, he commingled more and more genres, he calculated how to best assemble a band that could help him smash through the racial barriers of the industry, and he got to work fighting against the regressive approach of Warner Bros. to promoting black musicians.

"Prince was very concerned about being labeled a Black artist or being segmented into the Black department. He said to us, 'I'm not an R&B artist. I'm not a rock 'n' roller. I'm an artist and I do a wide range of music. If I deliver you rock 'n' roll, don't come back to me and say I can't do it because I'm Black,'" the Warner Bros. executive Marylou Badeaux was quoted in the 2003 book *Dance Music Sex Romance: Prince: The First Decade.*

By 1980 Prince had become a regular in not just the neighborhood he grew up, Near North, and the area where he attended school in South. He was clubbing all over the city, popping in to Sam's, which would soon become First Avenue, and the newly opened 7th St Entry to check out the latest dance, punk, and funk music, and living in a rented house off of Fiftieth and France, one of the bougiest neighborhoods in Minneapolis.

He wanted to assemble a band that could represent all of these different worlds, which only seemed to be growing further and further apart. "He understood the segregation of the industry. He said, 'I have to position myself so they can't treat me that way, they can't categorize the music that way,'" Prince's longtime manager Alan Leeds told the writer Touré in 2013. "'I have to have white people in the band and girls in the band. Sly had the right idea. I'm gonna do what Sly did and they're gonna cross me over, otherwise I'll forever be the Black artist.' He said, 'Whatever you do, don't allow yourself to be typecast in the R&B ghetto because then you'll forever be just that.'"

Whereas Steven Greenberg's "Funkytown" utopia was a far-off cosmopolitan city like New York, Prince set his utopia right in his own city. When he released the smoking-hot postdisco dance track "Uptown" in 1980, cowritten with his best friend André Cymone, Prince was proclaiming his hometown to be the freakiest, funkiest, most diverse place on Earth. "Black, white, Puerto Rican, everybody just a-freakin'," he sang in the song's chorus, concluding that "It's all about being free."

The song was an ode to the world where he and André grew up, even if his vision of it wasn't of this world. In reality, the Uptown neighborhood had a startlingly low 4.8 percent minority population, and the city was still grappling with omnipresent racial segregation. But if the real-life Uptown wasn't quite the multicultural epicenter that Prince imagined, he could sing about it and then make it so. He envisioned a world where blacks and whites, men and women, gay, straight, bisexual, straight-edge, and loose people could gather and party in peace. And much as the way he arranged his band into a utopian cross section of the human population, Prince reimagined Minneapolis into a world where he and his multicultural group of friends could achieve liberation.

Which ended up being a defining characteristic of Prince's work, and thus of the larger Minneapolis Sound movement: he was on an unending quest to wrestle himself out from under the oppressive

By the time Prince returned home in December 1979, he had released his second Warner Bros. album, *Prince,* and had gained a large enough following to perform at the Orphuem Theater in downtown Minneapolis. An advertisement for the show appeared in *Insight,* August 1979.

weight of racism and the restraints placed on him by the power-hungry music industry. And in order to truly find success, he had to figure out a way to incorporate that fight for freedom into his artistic aesthetic, until it coursed through everything from his band to his clothing (or lack thereof) to his electric fingers, which would sail across the fretboard of his guitar uninhibited and radiate his power out into the world.

While we can look back now and celebrate Prince's multicultural and multiracial bands as a sign of his progressiveness, in actuality it may have been a reactionary decision that he deemed necessary in order to succeed in a town and an industry he immediately recognized as racist. He knew the struggles that bands of his father's generation faced simply trying to play music downtown, and he knew the backlash that his friends in bands like The Family got for pushing their blackness to the forefront of their aesthetic. And most poignantly, he saw the overnight success that was afforded to a white peer from the very same setting who was making a similar style of music. Assembling a band with white members wasn't just an artistic or political statement: it was survival.

"Minneapolis was kind of like the last place, really, that discovered Prince after Warner Bros. gave it a pretty big push," says Bobby Z. "Obviously down South and the other regions where we ended up touring quite a bit later, they kind of got the whiff first, and got the sound first, then it exploded here. It was really a lot of fun to come home after those hits were on the radio."

Although Prince had made his debut playing material under his own name at the Capri Theater in 1979, he was still an unknown quantity to the majority of music fans living in the Twin Cities. Not only was it hard to find his music on the FM airwaves, but most of the area's white rock fans had their focus squarely angled toward the raucous, ravenous punk rock emanating from downtown's short-lived Longhorn Bar and the new 7th St Entry, a smaller room attached to a club known as Sam's, which would switch over in 1981 to the name that stuck, First Avenue.

The Suicide Commandos, the Replacements, Hüsker Dü, and Loud Fast Rules, which would morph into Soul Asylum, were all contributing to the explosive new scene, and their shows were complemented by more arty, experimental new wave sounds from bands like the Wallets and the Suburbs. Twin/Tone Records had become a force to be reckoned with and was cranking out releases from their Uptown offices, and the club concert calendar was filled with acts that would leave a scorching imprint on the Minnesota rock scene. Which made it the perfect time for the Twin Cities punk community to finally get around to checking out this gritty new Warner Bros. artist from their own city, who wore studded-up trench coats accessorized with Rude Boy buttons. He mixed up their edgy new wave with dashes of funk, dance, and blistering rock 'n' roll, and he seemed hell-bent on shattering not just racial but gender stereotypes, parading on stage with an electric guitar and high heels. After decades of musicians from his neighborhood struggling to play gigs anywhere near the center of downtown Minneapolis, it is striking that he broke through to the larger white community in Minneapolis by playing at a cherished downtown landmark that he would soon help draw stars around and highlight in bright purple on the national music map.

It was a Monday night at Sam's—March 9, 1981. A Monday night may not sound all that enticing for a concert, but Prince was riding high on the buzz around his most successful album yet, *Dirty Mind,* and "Uptown" had blasted up the R&B singles and dance charts and was bristling up against the bottom of the Billboard Hot 100 Singles chart—a sure sign that his crossover moment was finally imminent. Prince and his band, which consisted of André Cymone on bass, Dez Dickerson on guitar, Gayle Chapman on keys, and Bobby Z on drums, had been touring the country relentlessly, first on the underground Chitlin' Circuit opening for Rick James and then in larger clubs, selling out venues in cities like St. Louis and Chicago. The band was road-tested and ready. They had their dance moves and song changes choreographed to perfection, and yet they channeled the raw energy of punk rock and the in-your-face sexuality of the grimiest funk music, unleashing an unholy terror on the unsuspecting Sam's crowd.

Dressed in black stockings, cheetah-print briefs, and a flimsy white tank top, Prince commanded the crowd with a power he had only recently unleashed. It certainly hadn't been present when he nervously chatted with Dick Clark while making his television debut on *American Bandstand.* Even the well-crafted and genre-blurring material on his latest record couldn't possibly reveal how unharnessed he and his band would become live. "I knew from the second I saw him that I was seeing something magical and something special. This was really the first time, I think, Prince had found his audience in Minneapolis," said First Avenue house DJ Kevin Cole, during a radio tribute to Prince on KEXP in April 2016. "He came out and just blew everybody away. And what was cool was not only that, but I think he was blown away, too. You could see on his face and as he was playing, in the confidence, that he was also being fueled by this love and acceptance that he was feeling from the audience. That was really his coming out gig in Minneapolis."

The show received rave reviews and marked the first of several gigs that Prince would play at First Avenue in the 1980s, most notably including the night he and his band the Revolution debuted their songs from *Purple Rain* during a live recording in 1983. In 1984, when both the film and album *Purple Rain* would debut, Prince would catapult to the superstardom he had long craved. And yet he would keep his roots planted firmly in the soil of his hometown. Starting as soon as he experienced modest success with his Warner Bros. partnership, Prince would write and produce albums for his peers Flyte Tyme, revamping them into the Time; one of his earliest proteges, Sue Ann Carwell; his friends who would pursue solo projects, like André Cymone, Jesse Johnson, and Brownmark; and The Family, a name he chose as a callback to the band that nurtured him as a teenager in the early 1970s, though none of the original Family members would perform in it. And he would maintain a friendly rivalry with Jimmy Jam and Terry Lewis, who would leave the Time just prior to *Purple Rain* to launch their own chart-busting careers as producers and hitmakers, and who would be the first artists to produce number-one records across three separate decades with Janet Jackson, the SOS Band, and artists from the Twin Cities community like the Sounds of Blackness.

For all the commercial success, however, one of the lasting legacies of the Minneapolis Sound goes far deeper than album sales and tour productions. What is truly remarkable, in a city like Minneapolis, is that Prince and his peers would consistently perform their mixed-genre music to integrated and loving audiences, starting at that crossover show in March 1981 and continuing through decades of playing the most esteemed rooms and cavernous arenas in the metro area. "You can say all you want about me and my bands over the years, but you have to admit, we attracted the most diverse crowds to our concerts—blacks, whites, and people of all ages. We broke down a lot of barriers," Prince told *Minnesota Monthly* in 1997. Or to put it more succinctly, in the words of his dance hit "Controversy":

People call me rude, I wish we all were nude
I wish there was no black and white, I wish there were no rules.

Prince performed for the first time at Sam's on March 9, 1981, a date that would go down in history. Soon both the artist and the club would become Minnesota music icons, and Prince would launch the Minneapolis Sound into the global sphere. Photograph by Duane Braley. Copyright 1981 Star Tribune.

·

EPILOGUE

AFTER YEARS OF WONDERING about Prince, listening to Prince, collecting every record I could get my hands on that had anything remotely to do with the so-called Minneapolis Sound, and turning that sound all around and inside out, I finally got a chance to ask the man himself about how this city and space shaped him into the superstar he'd eventually become. Thirty years to the day after the best-selling album *Purple Rain* was released, I interviewed the drummer for the Revolution, Bobby Z, about his memories of meeting Prince for the first time and recording that pivotal album. I published it as a blog post for the radio station I work for, the Current, not ever imagining that Prince himself would read it. (Which is a lie, of course: writers almost *always* hope that artists read and care about what we write, even though they aren't the primary audiences for our work. And to write and work at a radio station in a city where Prince resided is to wonder, always wonder, whether he might actually be reading or listening.)

Later that afternoon, I got an email from Bobby Z: "P wants to know if you want to come out to a private celebration tonight."

I said, Yes, yes I did.

By this point I'd been writing about Prince for several years, but mostly from a distance: concert reviews, think pieces, interviews with his collaborators like Bobby Z, members of The Family, and artists from other various projects. The thought of actually speaking with him sent my mind reeling; I had several notebooks' worth of questions, yet after reading so many articles about his interactions with the media, I knew he'd frown on me taking notes or conducting a formal interview when we met.

When I got out of the car at Paisley Park that night, Bobby was standing in an otherwise empty parking lot, waiting for me. "I think we hit a nerve," he said, laughing anxiously. My stomach plummeted and hit the pavement underneath my combat boots. By the time a door had popped open and Paisley Park's longtime house manager and Prince's drummer, Kirk Johnson, welcomed us inside, I had practically reached a catatonic fugue state.

I don't know why Prince called me out there that night. Maybe it was a power play, or maybe he was just scoping me out. But what I do know is that after traveling out to Paisley Park numerous times and shuffling my feet around that building waiting for something, anything to happen, on this particular night there would be no more waiting or wondering. As soon as we got situated in Paisley Park's cabaret-style NPG Music Club Room, Prince emerged from the hallway to his studio, walked right up to me, and shook my hand. I introduced myself. He nodded, blinked his giant Bambi eyes, and peered directly into my soul.

For the next two hours, he flitted around me like a boxer, pressing me, teasing me, telling an endless series of jokes, and responding warmly and openly to any questions that I posed. In other words, he spent our entire visit completely disarming me and welcoming me into his world for a fleeting glimpse.

"I saw what you and Bobby did today," he said, walking me to his studio. What interesting wording: *what we did*. To write about Prince, it would seem, is not a passive act. What had we done? "I don't know why people have to do that, to look back on the thirtieth year of something," he said, studying my face for a reaction. "When else would we talk like that? What's the point?" He turned around to Bobby Z, who was walking behind us in the hallway. "Bobby, do you remember when we went to high school together?" he said in a high-pitched, shrill tone. He was mocking me, and I wasn't even mad.

"Why do people do that? I guess they don't have anything interesting happening in their present lives. I'm not interested in looking back. I'm too busy doing this." With that, he swung open the door of Paisley Park's Studio B, waving a hand in the air and wincing at the lights that were on full blast.

"Set a mood," he said to no one in particular, and suddenly the studio lights were dimmed and several candles were lit. We listened to several tracks off his soon-to-be-released albums, the solo record *Art Official Age* and a release with his rock band 3RDEYEGIRL called *PLECTRUMELECTRUM*. When he'd had enough, we stood up to walk back to the NPG Room and he fell in step alongside me. "Will you pay for that?" he asked, studying my face again. Without hesitation, I said yes, then asked, "What's the price?" He just smiled.

When we got back into the hallway, he seemed to want to linger near the photographs that are plastered on the wall outside, which are spread out in a timeline from the late 1970s through the late 1980s. Pausing by the year 1985, he pointed to his photograph on the cover of *Rolling Stone*. "See that?" he said. "They wanted me to pose for a photo shoot, but I was too busy, so they took a screen grab of my video and blew it up for the cover." He scoffed, and Bobby pointed out how pixelated it was, and how he had never noticed that before. "Look at my teeth, see these gaps? C'mon. They were obviously like, 'Fine, you don't want to pose for a photo? Here!' Brother ain't got no teeth!"

It was at this moment that I finally let out a big, hearty laugh, and Prince did, too. When he would tell a joke, he would jump back like he'd just set off a firecracker, run around in a little circle, and come back to see if I wanted more. We cat-and-moused it for a while in this way, giving each other a hard time, and I got the sense I was finally glimpsing a part of Prince that I'd long wondered about—that kid who grew up on the North Side, who treated his band like a gang, and who wielded his guitar like a weapon. That kid whose only goal in life was to show every other musician in town that they weren't shit. That kid who could rough you up on the basketball court just as fiercely as he could in the studio.

We started walking again. "I wanted to ask you about something, since you don't look back," I said. "How do you feel about the Minnesota Historical Society's photo exhibit, with all the Charles Chamblis photos? They have a very early photo of you with Grand Central, and the suit you wore with that band."

He stopped walking again. "Oh?"

"Yeah," I said. "And they have a picture of you at one of your very first gigs: you're in the background of a couple of runway models at a fashion show."

"Oh, that's okay. I'd like to see that!"

"It's really cool," I assured him.

"Cool," he said.

"What was it like back in those days?" I asked, knowing full well he typically refused to reminisce about such things. To my surprise, he was more than willing to answer.

"I saw this documentary called *The Art of Hip Hop* that talks about how they cut funding for all the music programs in schools and took away all the instruments, and record players were literally the only instrument left. You know the poverty is at an extreme level when all you have left is record players. It was never like that for us growing up."

"You had a lot of instruments available?" I asked.

"Oh yeah, we had instruments strewn about," he said, waving his hand in the air. "Saxophones and guitars and drums. I started on saxophone," he said.

"I didn't know that!" I answered.

"Yeah! I started on sax, but I had to quit because it was hurting my lip. Did you know Maceo [Parker]—I saw him just the other night—he has to have surgery on his lip because it's cut so bad? And Sheila E., if you ever shake her hand, her hands are ROUGH. She has tough hands." He mimed playing the bongos, then pretended like he was shaking Sheila's hand and running away.

"What kind of radio would you listen to back then? KQRS?"

"That's how I discovered Joni, Earth, Wind & Fire," he said. "I used to listen to it all the time."

"Did you ever listen to KMOJ?" I wondered, and he wrinkled his nose. "No. But before there was KMOJ, 89.9 was KUXL. I used to listen to that a lot."

By this point, Prince had invited a young guitarist named Darren

Hart (who performs as Harts) to the stage to perform a short set with Paisley Park's house band. Harts was Australian, and Prince had flown him up for a visit after discovering his music on YouTube. "He reminds me of how I was at that age," he said, obviously impressed with the young player's guitar abilities. "I want him to have the opportunity to play with real musicians."

The band struck up a jazzy, spare rendition of Bonnie Raitt's song "I Can't Make You Love Me," and I couldn't help but get caught up in all the events that had led to this very moment in time. The fact that Raitt had cut her teeth here in Minnesota all those years ago on Lake Minnetonka, that same body of water that Prince would make famous with a line about purifying one's self in it in *Purple Rain*. And the fact that he would embrace her song and cover it many times throughout his career, including on his 1996 album *Emancipation*. I wondered if Prince knew about Raitt's Minnesota roots, or if they had ever met or played together. There were so many more things I wanted to ask him, and I had no idea how much more time we would get to spend together. As the music swelled and Harts stepped forward to take a guitar solo, Prince reached out his hand and looked me right in the eye.

"Do you want to dance?" he asked, smiling.

Before I could react, he whipped his hand away. "Just kidding!"

As I burst into laughter, he hopped back like he'd just set off another firecracker at my feet. "No, really, do you want to dance?" And then again, before I could respond, "Just kidding!"

My face turned bright red, and I giggled and stared down at my feet. Before I could ask him anything else, he'd flitted off and disappeared into the night.

That North Side spirit still rears its head in all of those teenagers from Prince's Grand Central heyday. When Morris Day regrouped the original members of Prince's first side project after signing to Warner Bros., the Time, to perform a tribute in their leader's honor at the 2017 Grammys, it didn't take much to crack their cool facade and reveal their more playful, yet fiercely competitive personalities. Standing up at the back of the pressroom, the longtime *Star Tribune* music critic Jon Bream raised his hand to ask Day and the Time a question. Before he could get a word in, though, the entire crew melted and started slapping each other's backs at the sight of Bream. It was as if you could see them time-traveling in that moment to back before Prince passed away; back before the stress of being in the limelight and feeling the full pressure of the music industry had cracked their friendships apart; back before *Purple Rain* and the Time and Prince getting signed and Minneapolis getting turned on its ear. In that moment you could see them rabble-rousing together as teenagers, jockeying for that neighborhood notoriety, doing their best to one-up each another on a daily basis.

Jon Bream asked them what they thought about Bruno Mars paying tribute to Prince after them at the Grammys. Jimmy Jam—who sits on the Grammys board, is one of the most revered producers in contemporary music history, and presents himself as one of the most congenial and professional figures in the industry—nodded as Morris Day paid Mars lip service, but he couldn't help but let out a few words of truth under his breath. "We kicked his ass, though," he said, and the whole band let out one big, hearty, backslapping laugh and hightailed it out of the room.

I must state the obvious: the Minneapolis Sound has persevered and continued impacting not just the Twin Cities but the larger pop world for decades after the most famous players' careers exploded. Immediately following the signing of Prince to Warner Bros. in 1976, the artist started negotiating with the label to produce records by his Minneapolis peers. Starting with the release of an album by his friend and first protégé Sue Ann Carwell in 1981, carrying through the writing, recording, and release of the Time's debut the following year, and leading all the way up until a month before Prince died, when he jumped onstage with players like David Eiland (of Flyte Tyme) and Bobby Vandell (of Lipps, Inc.'s live band) to rip a guitar solo at their Ray Charles tribute show at the Chanhassen Dinner Theater, he seemed intent on using his fame to elevate his hometown peers and to exhibit his pride in them.

The words *Minneapolis Sound* had been explored by journalists in the Twin Cities starting as early as the 1960s, but it was in the '80s that the phrase entered the national music journalism lexicon. Albums by the Time, Vanity 6, André Cymone, Jesse Johnson, The Family, Mazarati, and Sheila E., not to mention the Jimmy Jam and Terry Lewis–produced hit albums by Janet Jackson, are widely regarded as the ultimate realization and expression of the Minneapolis Sound, known for its combination of synthesizers, computerized drumbeats, and electric guitars, and its dance-funk aesthetic. The success of the sound had become so massive by the end of the 1980s that the Twin Cities public television station produced a documentary investigating its impact, and Rick Shefchik from the *Pioneer Press* penned an article asking, "What's all this about a 'Minneapolis Sound'?"

As musical trends cycle through and people long to remember a simpler time, the vibrant, synthy dance beats and unparalleled guitar work continue to resurge. Bruno Mars is an obvious example of that legacy: his song "Uptown Funk" is named, after all, in honor of that bohemian Minneapolis neighborhood of yesteryear, and he quotes Morris Day in the line "I kiss myself, look so damn fine." But there are also traces of the Minneapolis Sound spread across the airwaves, from Justin Timberlake to Beyoncé to avant-garde R&B artists like Frank Ocean and Childish Gambino.

Remarkably, the musicians who helped pave the way for Prince's generation have also experienced a resurgence in interest, thanks in large part to a pair of deep-diving compilations that explore the roots of this intoxicating sound. In Minneapolis, the Secret Stash label released *Twin Cities Funk and Soul: Lost R&B Grooves from Minneapolis/St. Paul 1964–1979*. Their album release show was so wildly successful that the label spun off the excitement around the album to launch a second-act career for Sonny Knight, who later toured the country with the label's house band, the Lakers. And in Chicago, Numero Group continues to explore the lost demo tapes and limited-pressing releases from this era, reissuing the Lewis Connection's self-titled album, a collection of demos by Mind & Matter, and an expansive collection of deep cuts titled *Purple Snow*.

Let's keep it going. As more curiosity develops about the rich R&B, gospel, soul, doo-wop, blues-rock, jazz, and funk artists who laid the bricks to build the Minneapolis Sound, more and more stories are emerging from the players and fans who kept this underground scene alive, against all odds. Although this history stretches all the way back to the 1950s, it's a story that's far from over.

ACKNOWLEDGMENTS AND SOURCES

THIS BOOK WOULD SIMPLY NOT EXIST without the encouragement and constant attention of my wonderful editor, Erik Anderson. He was the first to plant the possibility of a music history book in my mind, and he held my hand through many moments of uncertainty and full-blown anxiety as I figured out how to unpack this enormous story. Thank you, Erik. I am so grateful to all the kind folks at the University of Minnesota Press who helped see this book to completion, especially Kristian Tvedten and Melissa Jones.

Thank you as well to my employer, Minnesota Public Radio's 89.3 The Current, who was extremely accommodating as I squeezed in all the hours of working on this book around my already busy job as writer, producer, and host of *The Local Show*. I'm sorry for every day that I showed up in the office looking like a zombie, but I assure you it's all been worth it. Also, I could not do half the things I do without the unyielding support of my husband, Ben Clark, whose love and encouragement saw me through many late nights and early mornings.

In terms of research, I owe a huge debt of gratitude to the Minneapolis label Secret Stash Records, whose 2012 compilation *Twin Cities Funk and Soul: Lost R&B Grooves from Minneapolis/St. Paul 1964–1979* was the impetus for this book, and whose detailed liner notes left a bread crumb trail for me to follow. Both Eric Foss and Will Gilbert were invaluable to this project and were incredibly generous with their time and knowledge.

To the librarians at my two favorite research facilities in the Twin Cities, the Minneapolis Central Library's Special Collections and the Minnesota Historical Society's Gale Library, and to generous researchers like Kirstin Delegard of Historyapolis—you all have the coolest jobs, and I thank you for your time and admire your work preserving the stories of our state.

Researching a period of recent history that spans more than two decades—and concludes two years before my own birth—was daunting. When I began, I recognized that this book would need not only the powerful stories of the musicians who shaped the scene with their own voices and hands but also the context of the social and political changes occurring in the Twin Cities from the 1950s through the 1980s. The sources I relied on varied wildly. You'll find most primary sources listed in the bibliography, but I wanted to call out a few in particular and shed some light on my process.

First I read every Prince biography I could get my hands on, including the out-of-print *Prince: A Pop Life* by Dave Hill, which delved further into the North Minneapolis R&B scene than most others, and the long-lost collection of early Prince interviews and biographical research by longtime *Star Tribune* music critic Jon Bream, who has been on the beat long enough to cover Prince's career from start to finish, called *Prince: Inside the Purple Reign.* Even though I considered myself relatively well-versed in Princeology after reporting on his movements here in the Twin Cities for the past decade, I wanted to make sure I left no stone unturned as I explored how he was shaped by his hometown.

Once I had a decent idea of where the story would end, I traced it back to the beginning. I scoured back issues of music magazines like *Connie's Insider* (later *Insider*) and read hundreds of articles from the daily newspapers (known in the '50s and '60s as the *Minneapolis Star* and *Minneapolis Tribune,* plus the *St. Paul Pioneer Press* and *St. Paul Dispatch*) as well as papers focused on the black community like *Minnesota Spokesman-Recorder* and *Insight.* I looked for articles about music, naturally, but also for any reporting I could find about the construction of I-94, the displacement of the Rondo community, the civil unrest of the late 1960s, the local government's often ill-guided attempts to counteract segregation and deter crime, and neighborhood community centers in Minneapolis and St. Paul. I pulled public documents from the City Council, dug up scholarly papers and theses from university students who had researched social and political changes in the Twin Cities, and sifted through the files of organizations like The Way, searching for clues. It was astonishing how difficult it was to find complete narratives of many of these historical developments, especially given how many parallels can be so easily drawn between what the cities of Minneapolis and St. Paul were grappling with in the 1960s and what we're still trying to figure out today.

And, of course, there were the interviews, some of them three or four hours long, with the musicians and witnesses who experienced the evolution of the jazz–gospel–funk–soul–rock scene firsthand. Through this process of collecting oral histories, I learned how important it is to sit back, stay quiet, and listen. To watch someone dig deep into their memories and see their eyes shimmer at the realization of a long-lost memory or discovery of an unexamined link between two seemingly disconnected experiences is both intimate and beautiful. It occurred to me that a nonfiction book such as this is entirely reliant on the willingness and trust of the subject's sources to open up and share these memories, and it was an honor to capture them as they came pouring out.

Not everyone I asked was ready or willing to go there, which is understandable, especially in the wake of Prince's death. Many musicians are working on autobiographies of their own and hoped to preserve their stories for their own projects, and I cannot wait to read them. Unfortunately, as is the nature of historical projects, not all of the central characters of this history are still alive to pass on their stories to future generations—another reminder that we need to collect these narratives and write them down in permanent ink while there's still time.

I am so appreciative of every single musician and scene witness who spent time sharing stories with me and opening their homes, hearts, photo albums, and scrapbooks. Thank you, thank you, thank you, especially to Lamar Munson, Howard Munson, Lance Grigsby,

Herman Jones, Willie Walker, James Martin, Pamela Parker, Willie Murphy, Maurice Jacox, David Hersk, Maurice Young, Nona Young, Monroe Wright, Sonny Knight, Wilbur Cole, Bill Gaskill, Pierre Lewis, Joe Lewis Jr., Jeff Tresvant, Ronald Bronson, Gwen Matthews, Wanda Davis, Sonny Thompson, Steven Greenberg, Bobby Z, Owen Husney, André Cymone, Katherine Copeland Anderson, Terry Jackson, Morris Day, and Prince.

Even with all the contributions from all these beautiful souls, there are still many unsung melodies out there waiting to be heard. This story could go on and on, and I hope it does.

SIGNIFICANT RECORDINGS

I T MAY SEEM OBVIOUS, as this is a music history book, but listening to the music was essential to my research. Specifically, tracking down and savoring music by pioneering Twin Cities R&B, soul, and funk artists in the 1950s, '60s, and '70s informed my understanding of how the Minneapolis Sound was realized. In an era where so much music is available on streaming services, it can be easy to forget that there are countless harder-to-find recordings out there that can help us to connect on a deeper level to the history of our communities and the evolution of the sounds we love.

Many of the essential recordings by Minnesota funk and soul artists have been reprinted and widely distributed by labels such as Secret Stash and Numero Group. Others may still be lingering in used 45 bins in antique stores and record shops, waiting to be scooped up. While this list isn't all-encompassing, it covers most of the releases that I listened to while writing this book and that helped me decode the *Sound* portion of the Minneapolis Sound. My list of albums ends in 1981, as I remained focused on the origins of the sound rather than its global reverberations in the mid-1980s and beyond, which has already been more widely documented.

ALBUMS AND 45s

The Big M's, "Silent Lover" / "Get Going" (1958, Laura)
The Velquins, "Falling Star" / "My Dear" (1959, Gaity Records)

The Wisdoms, "Two Hearts Make One Love" / "Lost in Dreams"
(1959, Gaity Records)

The Amazers, "It's You for Me" / "Come Back Baby" (1965, Bangar)

The Amazers, "Without a Warning" / "It's You for Me" (1967,
Thomas Records)

Dave Brady and the Stars, "Baby, Baby I Need You" / "Ridin' High"
(1967, Darby)

Willie Walker, "You Name It, I've Had It" / "You're Running Too
Fast" (1968, Checker)

Willie Walker, "A Lucky Loser" / "Warm to Cool to Cold" (1968,
Checker)

Maurice McKinnies and the Champions, "Sock-a-Poo-Poo '69
Part 1" / "Sock-a-Poo-Poo '69 Part 2" (1968, Black and Proud
Records)

Wee Willie Walker, "Ticket to Ride" / "There Goes My Used to Be"
(1969, Goldwax)

Jackie Harris and the Exciters, "Do It, To It" / "Get Funky, Sweat a
Little Bit" (1969, Black and Proud Records)

Maurice McKinnies and the Champions, "Sweet Smell of Perfume"
/ "Pouring Water on a Drowning Man" (1969, Black and Proud
Records)

Jackie Harris and the Champions, "Work Your Flapper Part 1" /
"Work Your Flapper Part 2" (1969, Black and Proud Records)

Wanda Davis, "Save Me" / "Take Care" (1970, Project Soul)

The Valdons, "Love Me or Leave Me" / "All Day Long" (1971, Twin
City Movement)

Haze, *Haze* (1974, Tektra)

The Philadelphia Story, "You Are the Song (I've Been Writing for
All of My Life)" / "If You Lived Here You'd Be Home Now" (1974,
Wand)

Prophets of Peace, "The Max" / "You Can Be" (1975, Maxx Records)

The Philadelphia Story, "People Users" / "Gotta Get Back" (1976,
H&L)

Band of Thieves, *Band of Thieves* (1976, Ovation)

Willie and the Bumblebees, *Honey from the Bee* (1976, Sweet Jane)

Morris Wilson, *Morris Wilson!* (unknown year, MoWil Records)

Bobby Lyle, *The Genie* (1977, Capitol)
Prince, *For You* (1978, Warner Bros.)
Bobby Lyle, *New Warrior* (1978, Capitol)
Morris Wilson, *Fantasy Island* (1979, MoWil Records)
The Lewis Connection, *The Lewis Connection* (1979)
Rockie Robbins, *Rockie Robbins* (1979, A&M)
Prince, *Prince* (1979, Warner Bros.)
Lipps Inc., *Mouth to Mouth* (1979, Casablanca)
Willie and the Bees, *Out of the Woods* (1980, Sound 80)
Sue Ann Carwell, *Sue Ann* (1981, Warner Bros.)
Prince, *Controversy* (1981, Warner Bros.)

COMPILATIONS AND REISSUES

94 East, *Minneapolis Genius: The Historic 1977 Recordings* (1985, Hot Pink Records)
Various artists, *Twin Cities Funk and Soul: Lost R&B Grooves from Minneapolis/St. Paul 1964–1979* (2012, Secret Stash Records)
Various artists, *Purple Snow: Forecasting the Minneapolis Sound* (2013, Numero Group)
Mind & Matter, *1514 Oliver Avenue (Basement)* (2013, Numero Group)
Flyte Tyme, "It's the Things That You Do" / "I've Got You on My Mind" (2013, Numero Group)

·

BIBLIOGRAPHY

THIS SELECTED BIBLIOGRAPHY lists the publications I directly referenced in the writing of this book. It is far from an exhaustive list of every document and article that I read or that is available on this subject.

BOOKS

Altshuler, Alan A. *The City Planning Process: A Political Analysis.* Ithaca, N.Y.: Cornell University Press, 1965.

Bream, Jon. *Prince: Inside the Purple Reign.* New York: Collier Books, 1984.

Cyrus, Barbara Sybil. *Minneapolis Negro Profile: A Pictorial Resume of the Black Community, Its Achievements, and Its Immediate Goals.* Minneapolis: Walter R. Scott, 1969.

Davis, Harry W. *Overcoming: The Autobiography of W. Harry Davis.* Afton, Minn.: Afton Historical Society Press, 2002.

Delton, Jennifer A. *Making Minnesota Liberal: Civil Rights and the Transformation of the Democratic Party.* Minneapolis: University of Minnesota Press, 2002.

Goetting, Jay. *Joined at the Hip: A History of Jazz in the Twin Cities.* St. Paul: Minnesota Historical Society Press, 2011.

Haralambos, Michael. *Soul Music: The Birth of a Sound in Black America.* New York: De Capo Press, 1974.

Hill, Dave. *Prince: A Pop Life.* New York: Harmony Books, 1989.

Lewis, Tom. *Divided Highways: Building the Interstate Highways, Transforming American Life.* Rev. ed. Ithaca, N.Y.: Cornell University Press, 2013.

Mumford, Lewis. *The Highway and the City*. New York: Harcourt, Brace and World, 1968.

Nilsen, Pers. *Dance Music Sex Romance: Prince: The First Decade*. London: SAF, 2003.

Plank, Raymond. *A Small Difference*. Great Barrington, Mass.: Vantage Press, 2012.

Robinson, Rolland. *For a Moment We Had the Way*. Andover, Minn.: Expert Publishing, 2006.

Shefchik, Rick. *Everybody's Heard about the Bird: The True Story of 1960s Rock 'n' Roll in Minnesota*. Minneapolis: University of Minnesota Press, 2015.

Touré. *I Would Die 4 U: Why Prince Became an Icon*. New York: Atria Books, 2013.

Vassar Taylor, David. *African Americans in Minnesota*. St. Paul: Minnesota Historical Society Press, 2002.

DOCUMENTS AND REPORTS

Ahmed, A. Karim. "Inside The Way." Pamphlet produced by The Way, Inc., February 1968. The Way documents, Minnesota Historical Society.

Cavanaugh, Patricia. "Politics and Freeways: Building the Twin Cities Interstate System." Prepared for Center for Urban and Regional Affairs (CURA) and Center for Transportation Studies (CTS) at the University of Minnesota, October 2006.

Davis, Syl. "In the Beginning." *The Way Newspaper*, 1, no. 1, August 17, 1968. The Way documents, Minnesota Historical Society.

El-Kati, Mahmoud. Historical statement, 1984. Archived documents from The Way. Minnesota Historical Society.

Futcher, Ruth M. "Plymouth Ave 1966–1967: Minneapolis' Experience with the Racial Violence and Riots of the Sixties." Prepared for University of Minnesota History Seminar 495: The '60s. Fall 1980.

Maddox, Camille Venee. "The Way Opportunities Unlimited, Inc.: A Movement for Black Equality in Minneapolis, MN, 1966–1970." B.A. honor's thesis, Emory University, 2013.

Minneapolis City Council. Meeting minutes for Standing Committee on Licenses, November 6, 1968.

———. "Petition opposing the closing of King Solomon's Mines, 114 Ninth St. So., as it would be detrimental to the cause of Human Rights." November 8, 1968.

Plank, Raymond; Arne Carlson; Jacob Bearman; St. Clair Beeman; Earl Bowman; Gladys S. Brooks; Charles McCoy; James McNeal; George Martens; Charles Stenvig; and James Butler. "A Report by the Minneapolis City Council's Commission on Human Development to the City Council and People of Minneapolis." August 1967.

Rosh, B. Joseph. "Black Empowerment in 1960s Minneapolis: Promise, Politics, and the Impact of the National Urban Narrative." Graduate thesis, St. Cloud State University, March 2013.

Stebbins, Robert Alan. "The Jazz Community: The Sociology of a Musical Sub-Culture." Ph.D. thesis, University of Minnesota, 1964.

"The Way: Arts Program, Workshops, Review." The Way documents, Minnesota Historical Society.

NEWSPAPER, JOURNAL, AND MAGAZINE ARTICLES

Balfour, Conrad. "Conrad Balfour on the Black Musician Problem." *Insider,* June 1971.

Bennett, Jim. "Jazz in the Twin Cities." *Twin Citian* VI, no. 7 (March 1964): 17.

"Bernadette Anderson, May 21, 1932—October 7, 2003: Queen Bernie." *Insight News,* October 2003.

Bernardo, Richie. "2015's States with the Highest and Lowest Financial Gaps by Race/Ethnicity." *WalletHub,* February 3, 2015.

Bream, Jon. "Funkytown Finally Rocks City Airwaves." *Star Tribune,* June 3, 1980.

"Civil Unrest on Plymouth Avenue, Minneapolis, 1967." MNopedia, Minnesota Historical Society. www.MNopedia.org. Accessed June 27, 2016.

Coifman, Jon. "North Minneapolis: Echos of the Unrest in 1967." *Star Tribune,* November 18, 2015.

"Council to Act on Liquor License." *Minneapolis Tribune,* January 9, 1969.

Cunningham, Dick. "The Way." *Minneapolis Tribune* (magazine), December 1, 1968, 41.

Graustark, Barbara. "Prince: Strange Tales from André's Basement (and Other Fantasies Come True)." *Musician Magazine,* September 1983, 54–63.

Greenbert, Jim. "Valdons." *Insider,* April 1972, 36–39.

Hill, Dave. "Maurice McKinnies." *Insider,* November 1972, 18–20.

Holbert, Allan. "Black Bands Abound, But Not in Downtown." *Minneapolis Tribune,* November 9, 1969.

Howell, Deborah. "Schools Face Race Shuffle." *Minneapolis Star,* July 9, 1969.

Jones, Will. "After Last Night." *Minneapolis Tribune,* October 19, 1968.

"KDWB Fabulous Forty Survey, Week Ending March 6, 1965." Survey courtesy Don Betzold, archived on oldiesloon.com/mn/ kdo30665.htm. Accessed January 2017.

Kaplan, Steve. "Local Bands: Dave Brady and the Stars." *In-Beat* 1, no. 5 (March 1966).

Kaszuba, Mike. "Plymouth Av. Community Reflects on Progress Made Since 1967." *Star Tribune,,* September 20, 1987.

Keller, Martin. "Portrait of the Artist as a Native Son: Minnesota's Most Famous Recluse Has Come Out of His Shell a New Man." *Minnesota Monthly,* March 1997.

Kissell, Ted B. "Prince's First Manager Reflects on the Music Icon's Early Days." *UCLA Newsroom,* May 2, 2016.

Klobuchar, Jim. Weekly column, November 1, 1967.

Manuel, Jeffrey T., and Andrew Urban. "You Can't Legislate the Heart: Minneapolis Mayor Charles Stenvig and the Politics of Law and Order." *American Studies* 49, no. 3/4 (Fall/Winter 2008).

Minutaglio, Rose. "Prince's First Music Teacher: 'He Was at the Band Room Door at 8 a.m. Sharp Every Day Waiting to Be Let In.'" www.People.com, April 26, 2016, accessed January 2017.

Murtha, Tom. "The Municipal Show Stoppers." *Insider,* April 1972, 13–18.

"Nightclub Called Trouble Spot." *Minneapolis Tribune*, November 7, 1968.

"Northsiders Confront Officials." *Minneapolis Star*, July 25, 1967.

Oldsberg, Jim. "Words of Wisdoms." *Lost and Found*, no. 1, November 1992.

Plank, Raymond. "Race, Poor Are Business Issues." *Minneapolis Tribune*, June 28, 1968.

"Police Aide Says '66 Race Strife Was Different." *Minneapolis Tribune*, July 21, 1967.

"Police Hold 10 in Raid to Find Drinking Minors." *Minneapolis Tribune*, October 17, 1968.

Powledge, Fred. "The Flight from City Hall." *Harper's*, November 1969.

"Prince Finds It 'Hard to Become Known.'" *The Centralian*, February 16, 1976.

"Proposal: Suspend License of Bar." *Minneapolis Star*, November 7, 1968.

Protzman, Robert; "Black Bands Let Music Talk for Them in 6-Hour Concert." *St. Paul Dispatch*, December 22, 1969.

Reicher, Matt. "The Birth of a Metro Highway (Interstate 94)." www.streets.mn, September 10, 2013.

"Sensitivity Survey Results." *Minneapolis Tribune*, November 18, 1968.

Shefchik, Rick. "What's All This about a 'Minneapolis Sound'?" *Pioneer Press*, July 24, 1988.

"Sound 80: In New Recording Complex." *Connie's Insider*, April 3, 1971.

Steele, Mike. "Herb Pilhofer Is Ready to Sound Off." *Star Tribune*, March 21, 1971.

"The 'Great White Way' in Downtown." *Minneapolis Tribune*, op-ed, November 11, 1969.

"The Minneapolis Riot That Wasn't." *Minneapolis Tribune*, July 21, 1967.

Walsh, Jim. "'The Highlight of My Life': Joe Minjares Brings Back Augie Garcia for a Rockin' Encore." www.Minnpost.com. May 19, 2015.

Wiese, Gloria J. "History of North Minneapolis." Youth Resources, www.youthresources.ws/history-of-north-mpls (accessed October 2015).

Williams, Chris. "Jimmy Jam and Terry Lewis Have Become Synonymous with Recording Excellence." *Wax Poetics* 59 (August 6, 2014).

FILMS

Hampton Alexander. Inner City Youth League, 1974.
Prince Unauthorized. River Road Entertainment, 1992.

PERSONAL INTERVIEWS

André "Cymone" Anderson
Jon Bream
Ronald Bronson
Wilbur Cole
Katherine Copeland Anderson
Wanda Davis
Morris Day
Bill Gaskill
Steven Greenberg
Lance Grigsby
James "Cornbread" Harris Jr.
David Hersk
Owen Husney
Terry Jackson
Maurice Jacox
Herman Jones
Sonny Knight
Joe Lewis Jr.

Pierre Lewis
James Martin
Gwen Matthews
Howard Munson
Lamar Munson
Willie Murphy
Pamela Parker
Prince
Bob Protzman
Bobby "Z" Rivkin
Sonny Thompson
Jeff Tresvant
Willie Walker
Irv Williams
Monroe Wright
Maurice Young
Nona Young

INDEX

Page numbers in italics indicate photographs and illustrations.

Andrea Swensson is a radio host and music journalist. Her weekly program on Minnesota music, *The Local Show*, is broadcast on Minnesota Public Radio's 89.3 The Current, and she writes for the Local Current blog. She has covered Minnesota music since 2005, formerly as the music editor of *City Pages*, and lives in Minneapolis.

Jellybean Johnson is the award-winning drummer of The Time. He has worked with a wide range of musicians, including Patti LaBelle, Alexander O'Neal, and Janet Jackson. He lives in Minneapolis, where he plays in The Jellybean Johnson Experience.